# Cooking
## for TWO

SHADY OAK PRESS

# Cooking for Two
## Efficient and Delicious Meals

Printed in 2008.

**Tom Carpenter**
Creative Director

**Jen Weaverling**
Managing Editor

**Kate Opseth**
Book Designer, Cover Design

**Stafford Photography**
Commissioned Photography

**Contributing Writers**
Melanie Barnard
Carole Brown
Mary Evans
Joyce Hendley
Tom Hyland
Patsy Jamieson
Jean Kressy
Karen Levin
Mark Scarbrough
Jill Van Cleave
Bruce Weinstein
Lisa Zwirn

**Special Thanks To:** Mike Billstein, Terry Casey and Janice Cauley.

**On the cover:** Grilled Pork Chops with Cuban Mojo Sauce, page 56.

**On page 1:** Warm Chocolate Truffle Tart, page 134.

1 2 3 4 5 6 7 8 / 13 12 11 10 09 08
© 2006 North American Membership Group
ISBN: 978-1-58159-370-9
Printed in China

Distributed by:
Sterling Publishing Co., Inc.
387 Park Avenue South
New York, New York 10016-8810

For information about custom editions, special sales, premium and corporate purchases, please contact Sterling Special Sales Department at 800-805-5489 or specialsales@sterlingpublishing.com

**SHADY OAK PRESS**

12301 Whitewater Drive
Minnetonka, MN 55343

# CONTENTS

Welcome     4

## SPRING & SUMMER Cooking     6

Dinner in a Flash     8

Dining à Deux     16

Spring Fling     24

Steak Medley     32

Summer Kitchen     40

Market-Fresh Meals     48

Suppers that Sizzle     56

Summer Suppers     64

Small Effort, Large Payoff     72

Fresh and Fast     80

## FALL & WINTER Cooking     88

Spice is Nice     90

Good for You, Too     98

An Intimate Holiday     106

Harvest Dinners     112

From Steak to Stew     120

Cozy Comfort Food     128

Warm and Comforting     136

No-Stress Dinners     144

Small is Beautiful     152

General Index     158

# WELCOME

*Come along on a recipe-filled journey
as we solve the culinary challenge of*

# Cooking
## for TWO

Cooking for two has never been easy.
Whatever your reasons for cooking small amounts
— your kids have left the nest, you don't have any in
the nest yet, it's time for a quiet dinner by yourselves, or maybe
kids, guests or crowds just aren't part of the equation — it has
always been hard to find recipes geared to creating great meals
for just a pair of people.

Sure, you can always adjust ingredient amounts, and fiddle
with cooking times and methods. But changing up recipes never
seems to work out as well as we home chefs hope.

No, cooking for two has never been easy. Until now.

*Cooking for Two* holds the key to preparing small-portion meals
easily and efficiently … and achieving wonderfully delicious
results. Here are over 100 superb recipes, each one geared
specifically to the challenge of cooking only small amounts of food.

Because most of us cook a little differently in warm and cold
weather, this book is divided into spring and summer cooking, and
fall and winter cooking. Main dishes, side dishes, appetizers and
salads … it's all waiting for you in the themed sections ahead.

Plus, each set of recipes includes a bonus dessert! These sweet delights
aren't always geared to two people … but who ever complained about having
a little dessert left over for later on or tomorrow, or to give to friends?

Enjoy meeting and conquering one of the culinary world's greatest challenges
with all the ideas, tips and recipes in *Cooking for Two*!

SPRIN
& SUM

# G MER

# cooking

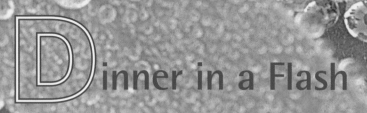

# Dinner in a Flash

*Skillet cooking is key to quick weeknight meals for two.*

## CHICKEN IN MOJO PAN SAUCE

*Mojo is a garlicky citrus vinaigrette that's a staple of Cuban cooking. While it's the perfect complement to these chicken breasts, it also adds a lively zip to shrimp or pork chops.*

2 boneless skinless chicken breast halves

¼ teaspoon plus ⅛ teaspoon salt, divided

¼ teaspoon plus ⅛ teaspoon freshly ground pepper, divided

1 teaspoon cumin seeds

2 tablespoons olive oil

4 large garlic cloves, minced

¼ cup orange juice

2 teaspoons lemon juice

2 thin orange slices

2 thin lemon slices

2 tablespoons chopped fresh parsley, divided

▶ Sprinkle both sides of chicken breasts with ¼ teaspoon of the salt and ¼ teaspoon of the pepper. Press cumin seeds into both sides of chicken.

▶ Heat oil in large skillet over medium heat until hot. Add chicken; cook 7 to 9 minutes or until golden brown and no longer pink in center, turning once. Place on plate; cover loosely with foil.

▶ Add garlic to skillet; cook and stir 30 to 60 seconds or until fragrant. Add orange juice, lemon juice, orange slices, lemon slices and 1 tablespoon of the parsley. Bring to a simmer, scraping up any browned bits from bottom of skillet. Stir in remaining ⅛ teaspoon salt and ⅛ teaspoon pepper.

▶ Serve chicken with sauce; spoon lemon slices and orange slices over chicken, if desired. Sprinkle with remaining 1 tablespoon parsley.

**WINE** A dry, fruity Chardonnay or Pinot Gris is perfect here.

**2 servings**
PER SERVING: 305 calories, 18 g total fat (3 g saturated fat), 27.5 g protein, 9 g carbohydrate, 75 mg cholesterol, 515 mg sodium, 1 g fiber

# BALSAMIC PORK CHOPS AND PEPPERS

*Using a variety of colored peppers brightens up this dish. The peppers also pair well with sautéed chicken breasts.*

10 oz. boneless pork chops, ½ inch thick

¼ teaspoon plus ⅛ teaspoon salt, divided

¼ teaspoon freshly ground pepper

1 tablespoon olive oil

2 cups sliced assorted-color bell peppers

  (about 2 small peppers)

1 small onion, halved, thinly sliced

2 large garlic cloves, finely chopped

1 teaspoon chopped fresh rosemary

1½ tablespoons balsamic vinegar

▶ Sprinkle both sides of pork with ¼ teaspoon of the salt and pepper. In medium skillet, heat oil over medium-high heat until hot. Add pork; cook 6 to 8 minutes or until browned on both sides and no longer pink in center, turning once. Place on plate; cover loosely with foil.

▶ Reduce heat to medium; add peppers and onion to skillet. Cook 5 minutes or until vegetables are softened, stirring frequently. Add garlic and rosemary; cook 2 minutes or until onion and peppers are tinged with gold, stirring frequently. Stir in vinegar and remaining ⅛ teaspoon salt. Return pork and any accumulated juices to skillet. Cover; cook 1 to 2 minutes or just until pork is heated through. To serve, spoon pepper mixture over pork.

**WINE** Choose a spicy Syrah or a tangy and flavorful Shiraz.

**2 servings**
PER SERVING: 325 calories, 17.5 g total fat (4.5 g saturated fat), 31.5 g protein, 9.5 g carbohydrate, 85 mg cholesterol, 500 mg sodium, 1.5 g fiber

---

## DESSERTS FOR TWO

### Shortcut Strawberry Shortcake

In a small mixing bowl, use a fork to crush 1 cup strawberries with ¼ cup sugar and 1 teaspoon lemon juice. Stir in 1 cup sliced strawberries. Let the mixture stand for about 15 minutes or until juices form. Assemble the shortcakes by placing 2 giant soft sugar cookies on dessert plates. Evenly spoon the strawberry mixture over the cookies. If you're feeling decadent, top each dessert with another cookie, then finish it off with a dollop of whipped cream.

### Warm Rhubarb Sundaes

In a small saucepan, stir together 2 cups sliced (¼ inch) fresh or thawed frozen rhubarb, ¼ cup sugar and ¼ cup orange juice. Cover the pan and simmer over medium heat, stirring once or twice, 6 to 8 minutes or until the rhubarb is soft and falls apart. If desired, stir in 1 tablespoon orange liqueur. Let the sauce cool slightly, then spoon it over vanilla ice cream or orange gelato.

# PAN-SEARED STEAKS WITH MUSHROOM-COGNAC SAUCE

*This recipe calls for button mushrooms, but feel free to use any combination of wild mushrooms available, such as shiitake or chanterelle. If you choose shiitake mushrooms, remove their tough stems before slicing the caps. Cognac adds a nice sweetness but can be replaced by beef broth for an alcohol-free version.*

2 (4- to 5-oz.) beef tenderloin or New York strip
   steaks, 1 inch thick

½ teaspoon sea or kosher (coarse) salt, divided

¼ teaspoon plus ⅛ teaspoon freshly ground
   pepper, divided

2 tablespoons unsalted butter, divided

6 oz. sliced button and/or wild mushrooms
   (about 2 cups)

¼ cup chopped shallots

2 tablespoons cognac, brandy or beef broth

1 tablespoon chopped fresh tarragon

▶ Sprinkle both sides of steaks with ¼ teaspoon of the salt and ¼ teaspoon of the pepper. Melt 1 tablespoon of the butter in medium skillet over medium-high heat. Add steaks; cook 5 minutes for medium-rare or until of desired doneness, turning once. Place on plate; cover loosely with foil.

▶ Melt remaining 1 tablespoon butter in skillet. Add mushrooms and shallots; cook over medium-high heat 4 to 5 minutes or until mushrooms are softened and most of the liquid has evaporated. Stir in cognac, tarragon, and remaining ⅛ teaspoon salt and ⅛ teaspoon pepper; cook 1 minute.

▶ Return steaks and any accumulated juices to skillet, spooning mushrooms over steaks until meat is reheated, about 1 minute. To serve, spoon mushroom mixture over steaks.

**WINE** Try a Cabernet Sauvignon.

**2 servings**
PER SERVING: 320 calories, 20 g total fat (10.5 g saturated fat), 27.5 g protein, 5.5 g carbohydrate, 95 mg cholesterol, 455 mg sodium, 1.5 g fiber

# THAI SHRIMP STIR-FRY

*A skillet makes an excellent substitute for a wok, especially when cooking smaller quantities. Because stir-frying is a quick process, be sure to have all the ingredients chopped and ready to go before starting.*

10 oz. shelled, deveined uncooked large or
    extra-large shrimp
½ teaspoon curry powder
1 tablespoon peanut or vegetable oil
1 tablespoon finely chopped fresh ginger
2 garlic cloves, finely chopped
⅓ cup unsweetened coconut milk
1 tablespoon fresh lime juice
1 teaspoon grated lime peel
⅛ teaspoon salt
⅛ teaspoon freshly ground pepper
4 tablespoons chopped fresh cilantro, divided
⅓ cup thinly sliced green onions

▶ Sprinkle shrimp with curry powder.

▶ Heat oil in medium skillet over medium-high heat until hot. Add shrimp; stir-fry 1 minute or until shrimp turn pink. Add ginger and garlic; stir-fry 15 seconds. Add coconut milk, lime juice, lime peel, salt and pepper; stir-fry 30 seconds. Stir in 3 tablespoons of the cilantro and all but 1 tablespoon of the green onions. Stir-fry 15 seconds.

▶ Garnish with remaining 1 tablespoon cilantro and green onions.

**WINE** Opt for an off-dry white to help balance some of the heat of this dish. Or try a spicy, dry white.

**2 servings**
PER SERVING: 255 calories, 15 g total fat (7.5 g saturated fat), 23.5 g protein, 8 g carbohydrate, 200 mg cholesterol, 400 mg sodium, 2 g fiber

# OLD-FASHIONED NEW YORK CHEESECAKE WITH STRAWBERRY GLAZE

*Cheesecake can be wrapped airtight and frozen up to 2 weeks; thaw overnight in refrigerator and add topping before serving.*

**PASTRY CRUST**

3 tablespoons unsalted butter, softened

1 cup all-purpose flour

¼ cup sugar

Dash salt

1 teaspoon grated lemon peel

½ cup unsalted butter, softened

1 egg yolk

½ teaspoon vanilla

**FILLING**

5 (8-oz.) pkg. cream cheese, softened

1¾ cups sugar

1 teaspoon grated lemon peel

1 teaspoon grated orange peel

1 teaspoon vanilla

¼ teaspoon salt

¼ cup whipping cream

5 eggs

2 egg yolks

**TOPPING**

4 cups ripe whole strawberries, hulled

½ cup sugar

4½ teaspoons cornstarch dissolved in ¼ cup cold water

2 teaspoons lemon juice

1 tablespoon unsalted butter

▶ Heat oven to 400°F. Remove sides of 9½- or 10-inch springform pan from bottom; generously spread 3 tablespoons softened butter on both bottom disk and inside surface of sides.

▶ In food processor, combine flour, ¼ cup sugar, dash salt and 1 teaspoon lemon peel; pulse to mix. Add ½ cup butter; pulse until large crumbs form. Add 1 egg yolk and ½ teaspoon vanilla; pulse just until it begins to clump. (Don't allow dough to form a ball.) Wrap dough; refrigerate 30 minutes.

▶ To shape dough for pan bottom, use generous ⅓ of dough. (Refrigerate remaining dough.) With lightly floured heel of hand, pat dough into thin layer over bottom disk of pan. Trim dough to inside edge of rim. Prick dough all over with tines of fork to prevent puffing as it bakes. Bake at 400°F. for 7 to 9 minutes or until light golden brown. Cool on wire rack. (Pastry sides are prepared later.)

▶ In large bowl, beat cream cheese on medium speed until smooth and creamy. Add 1¾ cups sugar; beat until smooth. Beat in all remaining filling ingredients except eggs and 2 egg yolks. Add eggs and yolks one at a time, beating well after each addition. Scrape down bowl and beaters; beat until smooth.

▶ Increase oven temperature to 500°F. If dough is refrigerated, bring to room temperature. To line pan sides with pastry, set springform ring on its edge; gently but firmly press remaining dough onto surface in an even layer up to ½ inch from top rim. Avoid getting dough into track that holds pan bottom. Fasten dough-covered sides to bottom disk containing partially baked pastry; secure spring. Set dough-lined pan on sturdy baking sheet.

▶ Pour batter into pastry-lined pan. Add 1 to 2 inches water to a 13x9-inch pan; place in oven on bottom oven rack to add moisture during baking. Place baking sheet and cheesecake on center rack in oven.

▶ Bake at 500°F. for 8 to 10 minutes or until golden brown. Reduce oven temperature to 225°F.; bake an additional 1 hour and 5 minutes to 1 hour and 10 minutes or until top is golden brown. Center should move slightly when pan is tapped, but will not ripple as if liquid. Turn oven off; remove pan of hot water, but leave cheesecake inside with oven door closed an additional 30 minutes. Cool cheesecake on wire rack, away from drafts, 3 hours or until completely cooled. Refrigerate at least 6 hours; cover and store in refrigerator up to 3 days.

▶ To make glaze, crush enough strawberries to make 1 cup pulp. Place pulp in medium saucepan; add ½ cup sugar and cornstarch mixture. Cook and stir over medium heat about 2 minutes or until mixture boils, thickens and is clear. Remove saucepan from heat; stir in lemon juice and 1 tablespoon butter. Cool to room temperature.

▶ Up to 4 hours before serving, remove cheesecake from pan. Arrange remaining whole berries over top. Spoon about ⅔ of prepared glaze over berries. Refrigerate at least 1 hour to set glaze. Pass remaining glaze as a sauce.

**16 servings**
PER SERVING: 535 calories, 37 g total fat (22.5 g saturated fat), 210 mg cholesterol, 290 mg sodium, 1 g fiber

# PORK CHOPS WITH TARRAGON-MUSTARD SAUCE

*This two-step, one-skillet entree is a boon when you need to get dinner on the table quickly. A vinegary mustard sauce makes the most of the flavorful pan drippings that remain after cooking the pork.*

2 (4-oz.) boneless center-cut pork chops

¼ teaspoon salt

¼ teaspoon freshly ground pepper

1 tablespoon olive oil

1 garlic clove, minced

¼ cup reduced-sodium chicken broth

1 tablespoon cider vinegar

2 tablespoons chopped fresh tarragon

2 teaspoons Dijon mustard

▶ Sprinkle pork with salt and pepper. In medium nonstick skillet, heat oil over medium-high heat until hot. Add pork; cook 6 minutes or until browned and no longer pink in center, turning once. Place on plate; loosely tent with foil to keep warm.

▶ Reduce heat to medium-low. Add garlic to same skillet; cook 15 seconds or until fragrant. Whisk in broth and vinegar; simmer 20 seconds. Whisk in tarragon and mustard. Return pork chops and any accumulated juices to skillet; remove from heat. Spoon sauce over pork; let stand 1 minute.

**WINE**  A Burgundy is an elegant choice to pair with this dish.

**2 servings**
PER SERVING: 260 calories, 16 g total fat (4 g saturated fat), 26 g protein, 2 g carbohydrate, 70 mg cholesterol, 460 mg sodium, .5 g fiber

# BLACKBERRY-GLAZED CHICKEN BREASTS

*These chicken breasts are dressed up with a simple glaze made with blackberry preserves. Make the glaze in the same skillet you use to cook the chicken; the browned bits left behind when the chicken is removed add another layer of flavor to the glaze.*

2 boneless skinless chicken breast halves

⅛ teaspoon salt

⅛ teaspoon freshly ground pepper

1 tablespoon olive oil

3 tablespoons blackberry preserves

2 tablespoons brandy, optional

1 tablespoon lemon juice

1 teaspoon Worcestershire sauce

▶ Sprinkle chicken breasts with salt and pepper. Heat large skillet over medium-high heat until hot. Add oil; heat until hot. Reduce heat to medium; add chicken. Cook 6 to 10 minutes or until chicken is no longer pink in center and juices run clear, turning once. Place chicken on plate; remove drippings from skillet, leaving any browned bits that cling to bottom.

▶ Place same skillet over medium heat. Add preserves, brandy, lemon juice and Worcestershire sauce. Bring to a boil; boil 2 to 3 minutes or until slightly reduced. Pour over chicken.

**WINE** Shiraz (or Syrah) is a natural match for the blackberry sauce.

**2 servings**
PER SERVING: 290 calories, 10 g total fat (2 g saturated fat), 26.5 g protein, 20.5 g carbohydrate, 65 mg cholesterol, 240 mg sodium, .5 g fiber

---

## SIDES FOR TWO

These side dishes can help round out a meal for any duo.

### Mango-Glazed Green Beans

Glazed green beans have an excellent flavor and are very simple to prepare; they're a nice choice with the chicken breasts or the pork chops. Blanch 1 cup green beans in boiling water 2 minutes; drain. Toss with 2 tablespoons slivered almonds and ¼ cup warm mango chutney (warm chutney in microwave).

### Pimiento-Topped Snow Peas

Serve snow peas tossed with an easy pimiento dressing with the pasta or stroganoff. Drain 1 (2-oz.) jar pimientos. Toss with 1½ cups steamed snow peas, ½ teaspoon minced fresh ginger, ½ teaspoon sesame oil, ⅛ teaspoon salt and ⅛ teaspoon pepper.

### Roast Fennel with Olive Tapenade

Roasted fennel complements the snapper. Heat oven to 450°F. Trim 1 large fennel bulb; cut in half. Place on rimmed baking sheet; brush with 1 tablespoon olive oil. Bake 20 to 25 minutes or until tender. Top with 2 teaspoons purchased olive tapenade and 2 teaspoons grated Parmesan cheese.

# EASY BEEF STROGANOFF

*When you're cooking for only two, it's easier to splurge on expensive ingredients, such as beef tenderloin, which is the most tender cut of beef. Notice that it's only cooked for a few minutes; cooking it too long makes it tough. Serve the stroganoff over noodles in the traditional manner, or over rice.*

½ cup all-purpose flour

1 teaspoon salt

½ teaspoon freshly ground pepper

½ lb. beef tenderloin, cut into ½-inch-wide strips

2 tablespoons unsalted butter, softened, divided

1 small onion, thinly sliced

1½ cups thinly sliced mushrooms

½ cup reduced-sodium beef broth

1 tablespoon Worcestershire sauce

1 teaspoon Dijon mustard

3 tablespoons sour cream, room temperature

▶ In shallow dish, stir together flour, salt and pepper. Dip beef in flour mixture; shake off excess.

▶ Melt 1 tablespoon of the butter in medium skillet over medium-high heat. Add beef; cook 3 minutes or until brown, stirring constantly. Place on plate; loosely tent with foil to keep warm.

▶ Melt remaining 1 tablespoon butter in same skillet. Add onion; cook 3 minutes or until soft and fragrant. Add mushrooms; cook 3 minutes or until liquid is released and evaporated. Stir in broth, Worcestershire sauce and mustard; bring to a boil.

▶ Return beef to skillet, along with any accumulated juices; simmer 1 minute. Remove from heat; stir in sour cream.

**WINE** Go with a hearty, spicy red for this dish.

**2 servings**
PER SERVING: 415 calories, 24.5 g total fat (13 g saturated fat), 29 g protein, 20 g carbohydrate, 110 mg cholesterol, 800 mg sodium, 2 g fiber

# SNAPPER IN PARCHMENT

*Although this recipe may seem fussy, it's perfect for a weekday supper. Once you get the hang of creating the parchment cases, the fish cooks up quickly. You can find parchment paper in the aisle with the plastic wrap and aluminum foil. Serve the fish in the packets; snip them open with scissors at the table.*

> 2 (15x12-inch) sheets parchment paper or foil
>
> 2 (6-oz.) red snapper or other white fish fillets,
>   skin removed
>
> 4 teaspoons olive oil
>
> 12 oil-cured ripe olives, pitted, coarsely chopped
>
> 8 cherry tomatoes, halved
>
> 1 medium garlic clove, minced
>
> 2 rosemary sprigs
>
> 2 thyme sprigs
>
> 2 teaspoons dry vermouth, white wine or water

▶ Heat oven to 500°F.

▶ Fold parchment sheets in half to form 12x7½-inch rectangles. Cut into half-moon shapes, beginning and ending cutting at folded edges.

▶ Place fish on one side of each piece of parchment, parallel to crease. Brush fillets with oil; top each fillet with half of the olives, tomatoes, garlic, rosemary, thyme and vermouth.

▶ Fold paper over fish and toppings; crimp and seal edges securely, forming turnover-style packets. Twist and fold ends under securely. Place on rimmed baking sheet.

▶ Bake 10 minutes or until packets puff and fish begins to flake when gently pressed (press through parchment). To serve, place packets on plate; cut an "X" in top of each packet. Slightly pull back parchment.

**WINE**   The tomatoes and rosemary in this dish call for a red.

**2 servings**
PER SERVING: 285 calories, 14 g total fat (2 g saturated fat), 33 g protein, 6 g carbohydrate, 90 mg cholesterol, 355 mg sodium, 1.5 g fiber

# FROZEN CHOCOLATE CREAM SABAYON

*Chocolate is the focus of this creamy frozen dessert—the chocolate custard is topped with a warm chocolate sauce. It's like eating an intensely rich ice cream.*

### SABAYON

**3 egg yolks**

**¼ cup sugar**

**1 cup whipping cream**

**2 tablespoons dry Marsala wine**

**2 oz. bittersweet chocolate, finely chopped**

### SAUCE

**¼ cup whipping cream**

**2 oz. bittersweet chocolate, chopped**

▶ In medium stainless steel bowl, combine egg yolks and sugar; beat with wire whisk until light and creamy. Add ¼ cup of the whipping cream and Marsala; mix well.

▶ Place bowl over a saucepan of BARELY simmering water. (Bowl should not touch water.) Cook 7 to 10 minutes, whisking constantly, until mixture is thick and foamy and temperature reaches 160°F. to 165°F. Turn off heat; remove bowl. Add finely chopped chocolate; stir gently until melted. Refrigerate until cool.

▶ Meanwhile, line bottom of 4 (½-cup) ramekins with parchment paper. In medium bowl, beat remaining ¾ cup whipping cream until soft peaks form. Gently fold whipped cream into cooled chocolate mixture. Spoon into ramekins. Cover; freeze at least 4 hours or up to 24 hours.

▶ To make chocolate sauce, in small saucepan, combine ¼ cup cream and chopped chocolate; cook over low heat, stirring until melted.

▶ To serve, unmold frozen sabayon onto individual dessert plates.* Let stand 5 to 10 minutes to slightly thaw. Drizzle with chocolate sauce and serve.

**TIP** *Once frozen, sabayon can be unmolded, covered and returned to the freezer until ready to serve.

**4 servings**
PER SERVING: 450 calories, 35.5 g total fat (20.5 g saturated fat), 240 mg cholesterol, 35 mg sodium, 1.5 g fiber

*These dishes blossom for both of you with the unsurpassed flavors of fresh herbs.*

# GRILLED PORTERHOUSE STEAK WITH HERB BUTTER

*Porterhouse is the ideal steak to use when cooking for a duo because the cut is substantial and actually divides into two of the most tender cuts of beef: strip steak and tenderloin. You can, however, substitute any type of steak you prefer.*

1½ tablespoons unsalted butter, softened

2 tablespoons sliced fresh chives

2 teaspoons chopped fresh rosemary

1 (1- to 1¼-lb.) porterhouse steak, about
  1 inch thick

1 teaspoon olive oil

½ teaspoon sea or kosher (coarse) salt

½ teaspoon freshly ground pepper

1 tablespoon balsamic vinegar

▶ Heat grill. In small bowl, stir together butter, chives and rosemary; let stand at room temperature 15 minutes or until ready to use. (Flavored butter can be made up to 24 hours ahead. Cover and refrigerate. Bring to room temperature before using.)

▶ Brush both sides of steak with oil; sprinkle with salt and pepper. Place on gas grill over medium-high heat or on charcoal grill 4 to 6 inches from medium-high coals. Cover grill. Grill 8 to 10 minutes for medium-rare or until of desired doneness, turning once.

▶ Place steak on platter; immediately sprinkle with vinegar. Top with flavored butter.

**WINE** Cabernet Sauvignon works well with this steak.

**2 servings**
PER SERVING: 310 calories, 20.5 g total fat (9.5 g saturated fat), 29.5 g protein, 1 g carbohydrate, 100 mg cholesterol, 460 mg sodium, .5 g fiber

# GRILLED HONEY MUSTARD CHICKEN SALAD

*If you don't have an outdoor grill, the chicken breasts can be cooked using an indoor grill pan. Vidalia onions and grape tomatoes lend natural sweetness that balances the tart lemon vinaigrette and marinade. Serve the salad with crusty French rolls.*

2 boneless skinless chicken breast halves

¼ cup extra-virgin olive oil

2 tablespoons fresh lemon juice

1½ tablespoons chopped fresh dill

1 tablespoon honey mustard

⅛ teaspoon salt

6 cups mixed baby salad greens

½ cup thinly sliced Vidalia or other sweet onion

⅓ cup grape tomatoes

▶ With flat side of meat mallet, flatten each chicken breast to ½-inch thickness; place in small shallow dish. In small bowl, whisk together oil, lemon juice, dill, honey mustard and salt. Pour half of the mixture over chicken, turning to coat both sides. Let stand 5 to 10 minutes at room temperature while grill is heating. Reserve remaining oil mixture for dressing.

▶ Heat grill. Remove chicken from marinade; discard marinade. Place chicken on gas grill over medium heat or on charcoal grill 4 to 6 inches from medium coals. Cover grill. Grill 6 to 8 minutes or until no longer pink in center, turning once. Meanwhile, toss greens, onion and tomatoes with 2 tablespoons of the reserved dressing. Place on 2 serving plates. Slice grilled chicken across the grain; place on top of greens. Drizzle with remaining dressing.

**2 servings**
PER SERVING: 345 calories, 21.5 g total fat (3.5 g saturated fat), 30 g protein, 9 g carbohydrate, 75 mg cholesterol, 170 mg sodium, 4.5 g fiber

## DRESSING UP STEAMED VEGETABLES

Vegetables are at their best when lightly steamed, then dressed with a fresh herb topping. Good herbs for vegetables are tarragon, chives, thyme, marjoram, oregano, dill and basil.

### Herbed Butter

Stir 2 teaspoons of chopped fresh herbs and a dash each of salt and freshly ground pepper into 1 tablespoon of softened unsalted butter. For Herbed Citrus Butter, add ½ teaspoon grated orange or lemon peel to the herb mixture. Let the butter stand 15 minutes at room temperature before using, or refrigerate up to 24 hours. Bring to room temperature before using.

### Herbed Crumbs

In a small skillet over medium heat, toss 3 tablespoons of fresh French bread crumbs in 1 tablespoon of melted unsalted butter 2 to 3 minutes or until the crumbs are golden and fragrant. Stir in 2 teaspoons of chopped fresh herbs and a dash each of salt and freshly ground pepper. Use immediately.

### Herbed Olive Oil Vinaigrette

Stir 2 teaspoons of chopped fresh herbs and 1 teaspoon of white wine vinegar or lemon juice into 1 tablespoon of fruity olive oil. Let the vinaigrette stand at room temperature 15 minutes before using.

# ROAST RACK OF LAMB IN PARSLEY–THYME CRUST

*Ask the butcher to trim and french the lamb (cut the meat and fat away from the bones) for a prettier presentation and to make it easier to carve into ribs. Use a food processor to make homemade bread crumbs out of day-old bread.*

1 (1- to 1¼-lb.) rack of lamb

1 garlic clove, halved

2 tablespoons Dijon mustard

⅓ cup unseasoned fresh bread crumbs
  (preferably from French bread)

3 tablespoons finely chopped shallots

3 tablespoons chopped fresh parsley

1 tablespoon chopped fresh thyme

¼ teaspoon freshly ground pepper

▶ Heat oven to 425°F. Rub lamb all over with cut side of garlic. Place lamb, fat side up, in small shallow roasting pan. Spread top with mustard.

▶ In small bowl, toss together bread crumbs, shallots, parsley, thyme and pepper. Pat onto mustard mixture (crumb layer will be quite thick).

▶ Bake 25 to 35 minutes for medium-rare (internal temperature should reach 130°F. to 135°F.) or until of desired doneness (crumbs should be richly browned). Cover loosely with foil; let stand 10 minutes.

▶ To serve, carve between ribs. Arrange ribs, overlapping, on 2 serving plates.

**WINE** Merlot and lamb are a classic pairing.

**2 servings**
PER SERVING: 290 calories, 13 g total fat (4.5 g saturated fat), 25.5 g protein, 16.5 g carbohydrate, 75 mg cholesterol, 600 mg sodium, 1.5 g fiber

# CHESAPEAKE BAY CRAB CAKES WITH HERBED TARTAR SAUCE

*Light and fluffy, with a slight spiciness, these crab cakes were a hit in our test kitchen. Refrigerated pasteurized crabmeat is a fine choice here, although fresh or good-quality canned crabmeat also can be used.*

½ cup mayonnaise, divided

4 tablespoons finely chopped red bell pepper, divided

4 tablespoons finely chopped green onions, divided

1 tablespoon chopped fresh tarragon

1 tablespoon white wine vinegar (preferably tarragon-flavored)

¾ teaspoon seafood seasoning, such as Old Bay

½ teaspoon Worcestershire sauce

⅛ teaspoon hot pepper sauce

¾ cup panko or unseasoned dry bread crumbs, divided*

1 (6-oz.) container refrigerated pasteurized or canned lump crabmeat, drained**

2 tablespoons vegetable oil

▶ In small bowl, stir together ¼ cup of the mayonnaise, 1 tablespoon of the red bell pepper, 1 tablespoon of the green onions, tarragon and vinegar. Refrigerate at least 10 minutes to blend flavors.

▶ In large bowl, stir together remaining ¼ cup mayonnaise, 3 tablespoons bell pepper, 3 tablespoons green onions, seafood seasoning, Worcestershire sauce, hot pepper sauce and half of the bread crumbs. Gently stir in crabmeat. Spread remaining bread crumbs on plate.

▶ Divide crab mixture into 4 parts; form each into ½-inch-thick patty. (Crab cakes will be loosely packed.) Carefully dip crab cakes into bread crumbs to coat completely; place in single layer on another plate. Refrigerate at least 10 minutes to help cakes keep their shape.

▶ Heat oil in large skillet over medium heat until hot. Add crab cakes; cook 10 to 12 minutes or until rich golden brown on both sides. Serve with herbed tartar sauce.

TIPS *Panko are coarse Japanese-style bread crumbs usually found next to other bread crumbs in the supermarket.

**Refrigerated pasteurized lump crabmeat can be found in the refrigerator case in the meat and seafood department. It comes in a can but must be refrigerated.

WINE The herbed tartar sauce and crab need a rich Sauvignon Blanc with light herbal flavors.

**2 servings**
PER SERVING: 690 calories, 60 g total fat (9 g saturated fat), 19.5 g protein, 20 g carbohydrate, 110 mg cholesterol, 970 mg sodium, 1.5 g fiber

# BUMBLEBERRY PIE

*We chose the name "bumbleberry" for this pie because it uses a variety of berries.*

### CRUST
**Pie crust for double-crust pie**

### FILLING
**1 cup blackberries**
**1 cup blueberries**
**1 cup raspberries**
**1 cup sliced rhubarb**
**1 cup sliced strawberries**
**1 cup sugar**
**⅓ cup all-purpose flour**
**1 tablespoon lemon juice**

▶ Heat oven to 400°F. Line 9-inch pie plate with one crust.

▶ In large bowl, combine blackberries, blueberries, raspberries, sliced rhubarb, sliced strawberries, sugar, flour and lemon juice; stir gently to mix. Spoon filling into crust. Top with second crust; seal edges and flute. Cut slits in several places in top crust to vent. Place pie on baking sheet.

▶ Bake 50 to 60 minutes or until golden brown. If pie crust appears to be browning too quickly, cover edges with foil to protect crust. Cool on wire rack.

**6 servings**
PER SERVING: 420 calories, 14.5 g total fat (3.5 g saturated fat), 4.5 g protein, 71 g carbohydrate, 0 mg cholesterol, 275 mg sodium, 5 g fiber

## GUIDE TO RHUBARB

There are many varieties of rhubarb (which is a vegetable, not a fruit), from the greenish-pink Victoria to the intensely ruby Crimson red. Cooks vary in their preferences for field- or hothouse-grown plants, and choice is often determined by what's available in a specific area. All varieties contribute a pleasantly tart taste that needs to be balanced by the addition of a sweetener. For best results, keep the following tips in mind:

### Tender Stalks

The slenderness or plumpness of the stalks is not an indicator of tenderness; instead, look for firm, unblemished stalks without woody ends.

### Dangerous Leaves

Rhubarb leaves should never be eaten because they are toxic. Be sure to discard the leaves before storing and using the stalks.

### Brief Storage

Rhubarb is best used within a few days and should be stored in the refrigerator in a loose plastic bag. Before use, trim the ends and wash the stalks to remove any residual grit.

# Steak Medley

*Springtime flavors infuse these steak dishes tailored for two.*

## HALIBUT STEAK WITH LEMON GLAZE

*Halibut steaks have a bone in the center and skin that circles the flesh. They're thicker and sturdier than fillets, which makes them a better choice for cooking in a grill pan. Ask your fishmonger for half of a full steak, which contains two meaty portions. After the fish is cooked, the two steaks will separate easily from the bone and skin.*

> 1 tablespoon grated lemon peel
> ¼ cup fresh lemon juice
> 1 tablespoon sugar
> 1 lb. halibut steak (1 inch thick)
> ¼ teaspoon kosher (coarse) salt
> ⅛ teaspoon freshly ground pepper

▶ In shallow dish large enough to hold halibut, stir together lemon peel, lemon juice and sugar. Add halibut; marinate 10 minutes, turning fish a few times.

▶ Lightly spray ridged grill pan or large pan with nonstick cooking spray; heat over medium-high heat until hot. Remove halibut from marinade; reserve marinade. Sprinkle halibut with salt and pepper. Place on grill pan; cook 8 to 10 minutes or until halibut just begins to flake, turning once.

▶ Meanwhile, pour reserved marinade into small saucepan. Bring to a boil over medium-high heat. Reduce heat to low; simmer 2 minutes. Serve glaze over halibut.

**WINE** This meaty, lemon-accented fish needs a rich Chardonnay.

**2 servings**
PER SERVING: 200 calories, 2.5 g total fat (.5 g saturated fat), 35 g protein, 9 g carbohydrate, 100 mg cholesterol, 355 mg sodium, .5 g fiber

# CHICKEN WITH OLIVES, TOMATOES AND PARSLEY

*This dish offers a taste of Provence, with its delicious combination of tomatoes, olives, garlic and onions.*

**2 boneless skinless chicken breast halves**

**½ teaspoon kosher (coarse) salt**

**1½ tablespoons olive oil, divided**

**1 medium onion, chopped**

**2 garlic cloves, minced**

**1 (14.5-oz.) can diced tomatoes**

**½ cup reduced-sodium chicken broth**

**1 tablespoon balsamic vinegar**

**½ teaspoon dried oregano**

**⅓ cup chopped pitted Kalamata olives**

**1 tablespoon capers, drained**

**1 tablespoon chopped fresh parsley**

▶ Place chicken breasts between 2 pieces of plastic wrap; with flat side of meat mallet, pound chicken to ½-inch thickness. Sprinkle with salt. Heat 1 tablespoon of the oil in large skillet over medium-high heat until hot. Add chicken; cook 5 to 7 minutes or until golden brown, turning once. Place on plate.

▶ Heat remaining ½ tablespoon oil in same skillet over medium heat until hot. Add onion; cook 3 minutes or until onion begins to soften, stirring frequently. Add garlic; cook 30 seconds or until fragrant. Add tomatoes, broth, vinegar and oregano. Increase heat to medium-high; cook 5 minutes or until slightly thickened, stirring to scrape up any browned bits from bottom of skillet. Stir in olives and capers.

▶ Return chicken and any accumulated juices to skillet. Reduce heat to medium-low; simmer 2 to 4 minutes or until chicken is no longer pink in center. Sprinkle with parsley.

**WINE** Red wine is a good match because of the tomatoes. Try one that's lighter in style, such as Syrah or Chianti.

**2 servings**
PER SERVING: 335 calories, 17 g total fat (3 g saturated fat), 30.5 g protein, 17.5 g carbohydrate, 75 mg cholesterol, 1210 mg sodium, 4 g fiber

# ASPARAGUS-GOAT CHEESE OMELET

*Tarragon and asparagus team up in a made-for-spring omelet. For best results, use a sturdy non-stick skillet with a flat bottom and sloping sides.*

1½ tablespoons unsalted butter, divided

8 asparagus spears, cut into 1-inch pieces

5 eggs

¼ teaspoon kosher (coarse) salt

1½ oz. soft goat cheese, crumbled

1 tablespoon chopped fresh tarragon

⅛ teaspoon freshly ground pepper

▶ Melt 1 tablespoon of the butter in large nonstick skillet over medium heat. Add asparagus; cook 4 minutes or until crisp-tender, stirring occasionally. Place on plate.

▶ In medium bowl, whisk together eggs and salt until light and foamy. Melt remaining ½ tablespoon butter in same skillet over medium heat until foamy, swirling to coat pan. Add egg mixture. As soon as bottom is set (about 30 seconds), slide thin rubber spatula under eggs. Push edges toward center, tilting pan to let uncooked eggs flow underneath. When top of eggs is almost set but still a little moist, place asparagus and goat cheese on one half of the eggs; sprinkle with tarragon and pepper. Fold omelet in half to cover filling. Slide onto plate; divide in half.

**WINE** Pair this egg dish with a rich, dry white.

**2 servings**
PER SERVING: 345 calories, 26.5 g total fat (12.5 g saturated fat), 21.5 g protein, 5 g carbohydrate, 565 mg cholesterol, 435 mg sodium, 1 g fiber

## ICE CREAM DESSERTS FOR TWO

### Vanilla Ice Cream with Broiled Pineapple

Cut half a cored fresh pineapple into ¾-inch slices; place on foil-lined baking sheet. Sprinkle with 2 tablespoons brown sugar; sprinkle lightly with ground cinnamon. Broil 8 to 12 minutes or until golden brown. Cut slices into chunks; serve over vanilla ice cream scooped into edible waffle bowls.

### Coffee Ice Cream Cookie Cake

Line 5x3x2-inch mini loaf pan with foil, letting extra foil hang over edges. Spread 1 cup softened coffee ice cream into pan. Cover with ¼ cup chocolate cookie crumbs; drizzle with ¼ cup fudge sauce.

Layer with 1 cup coffee ice cream and ¼ cup chocolate cookie crumbs. Fold foil over, pressing down gently to pack layers; freeze for at least 3 hours. Unmold onto plate; slice.

### Strawberry-Orange Sundaes

Peel 1 navel orange; remove segments between membranes. Thinly slice 1 cup strawberries. In small bowl, toss together orange slices, sliced strawberries, 2 tablespoons Grand Marnier or orange juice and 1 tablespoon sugar. Let stand 15 minutes, or make ahead and refrigerate. Spoon fruit and juices over scoops of strawberry ice cream.

# SPICE-GRILLED SIRLOIN STEAKS

*These very quick steaks get a fabulous spicy-smoky flavor from the rub. New York strip steaks, a very tender cut of beef, also are known as shell steaks, strip steaks or Delmonico steaks.*

| | |
|---|---|
| 1 garlic clove, minced | ½ teaspoon kosher (coarse) salt |
| 1 tablespoon lime juice | ⅛ teaspoon freshly ground pepper |
| 2 teaspoons chili powder | 2 New York strip steaks |
| ½ teaspoon ground coriander | (1 inch thick) |

▶ In small bowl, stir together garlic, lime juice, chili powder, coriander, salt and pepper. Spread over both sides of steaks. Cover and refrigerate at least 30 minutes or up to 1 hour. Heat grill. Place steaks on gas grill over medium heat or on charcoal grill 4 to 6 inches from medium coals; cover grill. Grill 8 to 10 minutes for medium-rare or until of desired doneness, turning once.

**WINE** Cabernet Sauvignon can stand up to the spice in these steaks.

**2 servings**
PER SERVING: 365 calories, 16.5 g total fat (6 g saturated fat), 50 g protein, 2.5 g carbohydrate, 130 mg cholesterol, 535 mg sodium, 1 g fiber

# PAN-ROASTED LAMB CHOPS

*The flavor that rich, tender lamb gets from a simple coating of Dijon mustard, rosemary and garlic is amazing! Lamb chops from the loin are small and thick and resemble miniature T-bone steaks.*

| | |
|---|---|
| 1 large garlic clove, minced | ¼ teaspoon kosher (coarse) salt |
| 2 tablespoons olive oil, divided | ⅛ teaspoon freshly ground pepper |
| 1½ tablespoons Dijon mustard | 4 lamb loin chops (1¼ inches thick) |
| 2 teaspoons chopped fresh rosemary | ⅓ cup unseasoned dry bread crumbs |

▶ Heat oven to 375°F. In small bowl, stir together garlic, ½ tablespoon of the oil, mustard, rosemary, salt and pepper. Spread over both sides of lamb chops. Place bread crumbs on plate; press both sides of lamb into bread crumbs.

▶ Heat remaining 1½ tablespoons oil in large ovenproof skillet over medium-high heat until hot. Add lamb; cook 3 minutes or until browned on bottom. Turn lamb; place skillet in oven. Bake 6 to 8 minutes for medium-rare or until of desired doneness.

**2 servings**
PER SERVING: 440 calories, 26.5 g total fat (6 g saturated fat), 37.5 g protein, 11.5 g carbohydrate, 115 mg cholesterol, 680 mg sodium, .5 g fiber

Spice-Grilled Sirloin Steaks

# LEMON MERINGUE PIE

*Sweet yet tart; it's no wonder Lemon Meringue Pie is so popular. To help ensure the perfect meringue, we've added cornstarch to the egg whites to stabilize the meringue, making it less likely to bead up or shrink from the edges during baking.*

**FILLING**

**2 eggs**

**4 egg yolks**

**¼ teaspoon salt**

**1¼ cups sugar**

**⅓ cup cornstarch**

**1½ cups water**

**¼ cup unsalted butter, cut up, softened**

**2 teaspoons grated lemon peel**

**½ cup fresh lemon juice**

**MERINGUE**

**⅓ cup water**

**1 tablespoon cornstarch**

**4 egg whites**

**½ teaspoon fresh lemon juice**

**Dash salt**

**½ cup sugar**

**2 teaspoons grated lemon peel**

**PIE SHELL**

**1 (9-inch) baked pie shell**

▶ Heat oven to 350°F. To make filling, in large bowl, whisk eggs, egg yolks and ¼ teaspoon salt until well blended. Set aside. In medium saucepan, combine 1¼ cups sugar and ⅓ cup cornstarch; mix well. Stir in 1½ cups water. Bring to a boil over medium heat, stirring occasionally. Boil 1 minute, stirring constantly. (Mixture will be very thick.) Slowly add hot cornstarch mixture to egg mixture, whisking constantly. Return mixture to saucepan. Bring to a boil over medium heat. Boil 30 seconds, stirring constantly. Remove from heat. Add butter; stir until melted. Stir in 2 teaspoons lemon peel and ½ cup lemon juice. Cover; let stand while making meringue.

▶ To make meringue, in small saucepan, combine ⅓ cup water and 1 tablespoon cornstarch; mix well. Bring to a boil over medium heat. Boil 30 seconds, stirring constantly. Set aside.

▶ In large bowl, combine egg whites, ½ teaspoon lemon juice and dash salt; beat at medium-low speed until egg whites are frothy. Increase speed to medium; beat until egg whites hold a soft peak. With mixer running, slowly add ½ cup sugar and cornstarch mixture. Increase speed to medium-high; beat until mixture is glossy and egg whites hold a stiff peak. Lightly fold in 2 teaspoons lemon peel.

▶ Heat filling over medium-high heat until very hot, stirring constantly. Pour into pie shell. Spoon half of meringue evenly over hot filling, making sure meringue covers all filling and touches crust on all edges. Spoon remaining meringue onto pie and spread evenly. Add decorative swirls with back of spoon.

▶ Bake 15 to 18 minutes or until meringue is dry to the touch and light brown. Place on wire rack; cool 2 hours or until room temperature. Refrigerate 3 to 4 hours or until chilled. Store in refrigerator.

**8 servings**
PER SERVING: 385 calories, 15 g total fat (6 g saturated fat), 6 g protein, 59 g carbohydrate, 175 mg cholesterol, 260 mg sodium, .5 g fiber

# Summer Kitchen

*Turn off the stove and fire up the grill for easy, relaxing dinners.*

## GRILLED MINI MEAT LOAVES

*Meat loaf mix is available in the meat department of most supermarkets. If you can't find it, ask the butcher to package it for you. The combination makes the best meat loaf: beef provides sturdy flavor and juiciness, while veal and pork add subtle nuances and tenderness. Serve the meat loaf with grilled potato slices.*

| | |
|---|---|
| **10 oz. meat loaf mix (equal parts ground beef, pork and veal)** | **1 teaspoon chili powder** |
| **1 small onion, finely diced** | **½ teaspoon dry mustard** |
| **½ cup fine fresh bread crumbs from French or Italian bread\*** | **¼ teaspoon salt** |
| **2 tablespoons chopped fresh parsley** | **¼ teaspoon freshly ground pepper** |
| | **1 egg yolk** |
| | **2 tablespoons spicy ketchup or barbecue sauce** |

▶ Heat grill. In large bowl, with hands, combine all ingredients except ketchup. Divide mixture in half; shape each half into free-form loaf about 4 inches long and 1 inch thick.

▶ Lightly oil grill grate. Place meat loaves on gas grill over medium-high heat or on charcoal grill 4 to 6 inches from medium-high coals. Grill 10 to 12 minutes or until no longer pink in center and outside is crusty, turning once or twice and brushing with ketchup. Pass additional ketchup to serve with meat loaves.

**TIP** \*To make fresh bread crumbs, tear 1 to 2 bread slices into 1-inch pieces; place in food processor. Process 30 to 60 seconds or until fine crumbs form.

**WINE** Opt for a spicy wine with this dish—a Shiraz (or Syrah).

**2 servings**
PER SERVING: 325 calories, 18.5 g total fat (6.5 g saturated fat), 28 g protein, 11.5 g carbohydrate, 195 mg cholesterol, 595 mg sodium, 1.5 g fiber

# CHIMICHURRI BEEF STEAK

*A juicy porterhouse steak is the perfect cut for two people, although you also can try another tender beef steak, such as filet mignon or boneless rib-eye. Italian parsley, or flat leaf parsley, has a stronger flavor than curly parsley. Look for bunches with bright green leaves.*

### BEEF

1 large garlic clove, minced

1 tablespoon chopped fresh oregano

¼ teaspoon kosher (coarse) salt

⅛ teaspoon crushed red pepper

1 tablespoon extra-virgin olive oil

1 (1¼ lb.) porterhouse steak (1½-inch-thick)


### SAUCE

½ cup chopped fresh Italian parsley

2 tablespoons finely chopped red bell pepper

1 tablespoon chopped fresh oregano

1 tablespoon red wine vinegar

2 medium garlic cloves, minced

¼ teaspoon salt

⅛ teaspoon crushed red pepper

2 tablespoons extra-virgin olive oil

▶ In small bowl, stir together all beef ingredients except steak. Rub mixture on both sides of steak. Let stand at room temperature 15 to 20 minutes.

▶ Meanwhile, heat grill. In small bowl, stir together parsley, bell pepper, 1 tablespoon oregano, vinegar, 2 minced garlic cloves, ¼ teaspoon salt and ⅛ teaspoon red pepper. Add 2 tablespoons oil; blend until combined.

▶ Place steak on gas grill over medium-high heat or on charcoal grill 4 to 6 inches from medium-high coals. Grill 6 to 8 minutes or until internal temperature reaches 130°F. to 135°F. for medium-rare or until of desired doneness, turning once. Let stand 10 minutes. Cut steak from bone; divide in half. Serve with sauce.

**WINE** Without question, this dish calls for a Cabernet Sauvignon.

**2 servings**
PER SERVING: 460 calories, 32.5 g total fat (7.5 g saturated fat), 37.5 g protein, 4 g carbohydrate, 95 mg cholesterol, 585 mg sodium, 1 g fiber

# GRILLED PIZZA MARGHERITA

*Because grilling time is short for this classic pizza, it's important to have all the toppings at the ready. Although you can make your own dough, prepared refrigerated dough works just as well, and one can is the ideal size for a two-serving meal.*

1 tablespoon extra-virgin olive oil

1 large garlic clove, finely chopped

1 (10-oz.) can refrigerated pizza dough

1 cup coarsely chopped plum tomatoes

⅓ cup coarsely torn fresh basil

⅛ to ¼ teaspoon crushed red pepper

¼ teaspoon salt

3 oz. thinly sliced fresh mozzarella

2 tablespoons grated Pecorino Romano cheese

▶ Heat grill. In small bowl, stir together oil and garlic. Unfold pizza dough onto lightly floured baking sheet. With hands, pat dough into rough 14-inch square; cut into 4 pieces. Lightly oil grill grate. Place dough pieces directly on gas grill over medium-high heat or on charcoal grill 4 to 6 inches from medium-high coals. Grill 2 minutes or until top is puffy and bottom is firm and golden brown with grill marks. Turn dough; quickly brush with oil and garlic mixture. Top with tomatoes, basil, red pepper and salt; sprinkle with mozzarella and Pecorino Romano cheese. Grill an additional 2 to 3 minutes or until bottom is browned with grill marks and cheeses are melted.

**WINE** This classic pizza calls for a classic wine—Chianti.

**2 servings**
PER SERVING: 620 calories, 28 g total fat (9 g saturated fat), 21 g protein, 75 g carbohydrate, 35 mg cholesterol, 1225 mg sodium, 4 g fiber

## GRILLED SIDES FOR TWO

### Grilled Potatoes with Malt Vinegar

Cut 2 medium russet potatoes into ½-inch slices. Brush the slices with 2 tablespoons of oil and sprinkle with salt and pepper. Grill the slices 5 to 8 minutes or until tender, crisp and slightly charred, turning several times; remove from the grill. Mix together 1 tablespoon malt vinegar and 2 teaspoons chopped fresh thyme, and drizzle over the potatoes.

### Gorgonzola Toasts on the Grill

Cut a small French or Italian bread loaf in half lengthwise; brush the cut sides with 1 tablespoon olive oil. Grill the bread, cut side down, for 1 to 2 minutes or until golden brown and lightly charred. Turn the bread; sprinkle the cut sides with 1 teaspoon chopped fresh rosemary, ¼ teaspoon pepper and ¼ cup crumbled Gorgonzola cheese. Grill

1 to 2 minutes or until the cheese is melted.

### Grilled Summer Vegetables

Cut 1 small zucchini in half lengthwise, cut 1 small Vidalia onion into ½-inch slices, and quarter one-half of a red bell pepper. Brush the vegetables with 1 tablespoon olive oil, and sprinkle with salt and pepper. Grill the vegetables for 5 to 8 minutes or until tender and lightly charred, turning once or twice. Remove from the grill; separate the onion rings and coarsely chop the zucchini and bell pepper. Sprinkle the veggies with 2 teaspoons chopped fresh basil, thyme and/ or rosemary, and drizzle with 1½ teaspoons balsamic vinegar.

# CITRUS GRILLED CHICKEN

*This marinade is a variation of the traditional mojo, a popular barbecue sauce in Cuban cooking. The various citrus elements and the cilantro are particularly well suited to chicken. Even though the marinating time is short, the breasts pick up a lot of flavor. You also can substitute boneless thighs or drumsticks.*

1 teaspoon grated orange peel

1 teaspoon grated lime peel

¼ cup orange juice

2 tablespoons olive oil

1 tablespoon lime juice

2 tablespoons chopped fresh cilantro,
   plus sprigs for garnish

½ teaspoon lightly crushed cumin seeds

¼ teaspoon salt

¼ teaspoon freshly ground pepper

2 garlic cloves, finely chopped

2 boneless skinless chicken breast halves

▶ In 1-gallon resealable plastic bag, combine all ingredients except cilantro sprigs and chicken. Add chicken; seal bag, turning so both chicken pieces are completely coated. Refrigerate at least 1 hour or up to 2 hours to marinate.

▶ Heat grill. Place chicken on gas grill over medium-high heat or on charcoal grill 4 to 6 inches from medium-high coals. Grill 10 to 13 minutes or until chicken is no longer pink in center and juices run clear. Garnish with cilantro sprigs.

**WINE** Chardonnay offers a lot of flavor that complements this dish.

**2 servings**
PER SERVING: 180 calories, 7 g total fat (1.5 g saturated fat), 26.5 g protein, 1.5 g carbohydrate, 65 mg cholesterol, 135 mg sodium, 0 g fiber

# FROZEN LEMON–LIME MOUSSE WITH BERRIES

*Individual molds of sweet-tart citrus mousse start with purchased lemon curd, a cooked mixture of lemon juice, sugar, butter and eggs.*

1 (10-oz.) jar lemon curd

1 tablespoon plus 2 teaspoons grated
   lime peel

1 cup whipping cream

4 cups raspberries

¼ cup sugar

1 cup blackberries

▶ In medium bowl, combine lemon curd and 1 tablespoon lime peel; whisk until smooth. In another medium bowl, beat cream until stiff peaks form. Gently fold cream into lemon curd mixture. Spoon evenly into 4 (6-oz.) custard cups. Cover; freeze at least 2 hours or up to 3 days.

▶ Meanwhile, in food processor or blender, puree 3 cups of the raspberries. Press pureed mixture through strainer to remove seeds; discard seeds. Stir in sugar and 2 teaspoons lime peel. If raspberries are tart, add additional sugar to taste. Cover; refrigerate. (Sauce can be made up to 3 days ahead.)

▶ To serve, dip bottoms of custard cups briefly in warm water. Run thin metal spatula around edges to loosen; turn out each mousse onto individual dessert plate. Smooth tops with spatula. Spoon raspberry sauce around each mousse. Garnish with blackberries and remaining raspberries.

**4 servings**
PER SERVING: 490 calories, 36 g total fat (11.5 g saturated fat), 65 mg cholesterol, 80 mg sodium, 4 g fiber

*Dinner gets a boost from the season's best produce.*

# GRILLED SIRLOIN STEAK WITH SWEET ONION AND BELL PEPPER TOPPING

*The sweet onion-bell pepper salsa served with this juicy, barbecue-flavored top sirloin elevates the meat from simple to spectacular.*

**1 (1-lb.) boneless top sirloin steak, about 1 inch thick, cut into 2 pieces**

**1 teaspoon purchased barbecue spice rub**

**1 sweet onion, coarsely chopped (about 2½ cups)**

**1 red bell pepper, coarsely chopped**

**2 teaspoons soy sauce**

**2 teaspoons vegetable oil, divided**

**¼ teaspoon salt**

▶ Pat steaks dry with paper towel; sprinkle both sides with barbecue rub. Cover and refrigerate at least 1 hour or up to 24 hours.

▶ Heat grill. Place onion and bell pepper on piece of heavy-duty foil. Drizzle with soy sauce and 1 teaspoon of the oil; sprinkle with salt. Seal packet completely.

▶ Place packet on gas grill over medium-high heat or on charcoal grill 4 to 6 inches from medium-high coals; cover grill. Grill 15 minutes or until vegetables are soft and tender, turning packet once. (Test for tenderness by poking small sharp knife through foil.) Remove from grill; keep covered.

▶ Meanwhile, brush both sides of steaks with remaining 1 teaspoon oil. Place on grill next to vegetable packet; cover grill. Grill 8 to 10 minutes for medium-rare or until of desired doneness, turning once. Place steaks on serving plates and cover loosely with foil; let stand 5 minutes. Top with warm onion-bell pepper mixture.

**WINE** Cabernet Sauvignon and sirloin are meant for each other.

**2 servings**
PER SERVING: 345 calories, 12 g total fat (3 g saturated fat), 47 g protein, 10.5 g carbohydrate, 120 mg cholesterol, 765 mg sodium, 2.5 g fiber

# CHICKEN WITH ORANGE, ROSEMARY AND NECTARINES

*Chicken breasts provide a wonderful foundation for the flavors of nectarines, orange juice and rosemary. A dab of butter blended into the sauce gives it a hint of richness. To add color to the table, serve this dish with a side of steamed broccoli.*

**2 boneless skinless chicken breast halves,**
   **lightly pounded**
**¼ teaspoon salt**
**⅛ teaspoon freshly ground pepper**
**3 teaspoons finely chopped fresh rosemary,**
   **divided**
**2 tablespoons all-purpose flour**
**1 tablespoon olive oil**
**½ tablespoon butter**
**1 nectarine, peeled, cut into 12 wedges**
**½ cup fresh orange juice**

▶ Sprinkle chicken with salt, pepper and 2 teaspoons of the rosemary. Place flour on shallow plate. Dredge chicken in flour, shaking off excess. Heat oil in medium nonstick skillet over medium-high heat until hot. Add chicken; cook 4 to 6 minutes or until golden brown and no longer pink in center, turning once. Place on plate.

▶ In same skillet, melt butter over medium heat. Add nectarine; cook 2 minutes or until softened and slightly golden brown, turning once. Place on plate with chicken.

▶ Add orange juice and remaining 1 teaspoon rosemary to skillet. Cook and stir 3 minutes or until reduced. Return chicken and nectarine to pan to heat through.

**WINE** Chardonnay is a fine match for this chicken dish.

**2 servings**
PER SERVING: 315 calories, 14 g total fat (4 g saturated fat), 28 g protein, 18.5 g carbohydrate, 80 mg cholesterol, 285 mg sodium, 1.5 g fiber

# PASTA WITH SPICY ITALIAN SAUSAGE AND MUSHROOMS

*Spicy crumbled sausage teams with fresh vegetables to produce a harmonious ragù. This meat sauce will be just as tasty if made ahead and saved for a busy weeknight. You can gently reheat it as the pasta cooks.*

4 oz. spicy bulk Italian sausage

1 small onion, finely chopped

1 small carrot, finely chopped

1 small fennel bulb, fronds removed and discarded, bulb finely chopped

1 (8-oz.) pkg. sliced mushrooms

½ cup grape or cherry tomatoes, halved

½ cup reduced-sodium vegetable broth or water

¼ teaspoon salt

4 oz. (about 2½ cups) shaped pasta, such as conchiglie (pasta shells) or orecchiette (little ears)

2 tablespoons grated Parmesan cheese

▶ Heat large nonstick skillet over medium heat until hot. Crumble sausage into skillet; cook and stir 3 minutes or until browned. Place on paper-towel-lined plate. To same skillet, add onion, carrot and fennel. Cook 5 minutes or until softened, stirring occasionally. Add mushrooms; cook 5 minutes or until vegetables are tender. Stir in sausage, tomatoes, broth and salt. Bring to a boil. Cover pan; reduce heat to low. Cook 10 minutes. (Sauce may be made to this point up to 2 days ahead. Cover and refrigerate.)

▶ Meanwhile, cook pasta in large pot of boiling salted water according to package directions. Drain, reserving 2 tablespoons of the cooking water.

▶ In large bowl, toss pasta with sauce and reserved cooking water. Serve sprinkled with cheese.

**WINE** Chianti offers stylish ripe fruit and spice.

**2 servings**
PER SERVING: 485 calories, 14.5 g total fat (5 g saturated fat), 24 g protein, 67 g carbohydrate, 35 mg cholesterol, 1155 mg sodium, 9 g fiber

---

## SALAD DRESSINGS FOR TWO

### Fresh Herb Vinaigrette

In small bowl, whisk together 1 tablespoon balsamic vinegar, ⅛ teaspoon salt, ⅛ teaspoon freshly ground pepper and 1 tablespoon minced fresh herbs (such as basil and chives or parsley). Slowly whisk in 3 tablespoons extra-virgin olive oil. About ¼ cup.

### Chunky Blue Cheese Vinaigrette

In small bowl, whisk together 1 tablespoon cider vinegar, ¼ teaspoon Worcestershire sauce, 2 drops hot pepper sauce and ¼ teaspoon freshly ground pepper. Whisk in 3 tablespoons olive oil. Stir in 2 tablespoons crumbled blue cheese just until combined. About ⅓ cup.

# PILAF-STUFFED EGGPLANT WITH MOZZARELLA AND TOMATOES

*This garlic-and-cheese-rich main course is ideal for a weeknight dinner because all the components can be made in advance. When ready to serve, just pop the stuffed eggplant into the oven and warm up the simple Italian-style sauce.*

**EGGPLANT**

1 small to medium eggplant (¾ to 1 lb.)

½ teaspoon salt, divided

1 tablespoon plus 2 teaspoons olive oil, divided

⅓ cup finely chopped onion

¼ cup long-grain rice

¾ cup hot water

⅛ teaspoon freshly ground pepper

1½ tablespoons prepared pesto sauce

4 oz. fresh mozzarella cheese, cut into 8 (¼-inch-thick) slices

**SAUCE**

1 tablespoon olive oil

1 garlic clove, minced

½ cup chopped seeded plum tomatoes

⅛ teaspoon salt

⅛ teaspoon freshly ground pepper

▶ Heat oven to 425°F. Line rimmed baking sheet with foil. Cut eggplant in half lengthwise. Make 3 shallow cuts in center of each half; place, cut side up, on baking sheet. Sprinkle with ¼ teaspoon of the salt; drizzle with 1 tablespoon of the oil. Bake, uncovered, 25 to 35 minutes or until tender. Remove from oven; reduce oven temperature to 350°F.

▶ Meanwhile, heat remaining 2 teaspoons oil in medium nonstick skillet over medium-low heat until hot. Add onion; cook 3 to 6 minutes or until soft, stirring occasionally. Stir in rice; cook 2 minutes or until rice is opaque. Add hot water, remaining ¼ teaspoon salt and pepper. Bring to a boil; cover skillet. Reduce heat to low; simmer 15 to 20 minutes or until tender. Remove from heat; stir in pesto.

▶ Without piercing skin, scoop out eggplant pulp. Return empty shells to baking sheet. Chop eggplant pulp; stir into rice mixture. Fill eggplant shells with rice mixture. Top each serving with 4 slices of the mozzarella cheese. Bake at 350°F. for 10 to 15 minutes or until filling is hot and cheese is melted.

▶ Meanwhile, prepare tomato sauce. Heat 1 tablespoon oil in medium saucepan over medium-low heat until hot. Add garlic; cook 30 seconds or until fragrant. Stir in tomatoes, ⅛ teaspoon salt and ⅛ teaspoon pepper. Cook 10 to 15 minutes or until tomatoes are very soft and juices evaporate slightly. To serve, place eggplant on plates; spoon sauce over and around eggplant.

**WINE** This dish calls for a red.

**2 servings**
PER SERVING: 550 calories, 35 g total fat (10 g saturated fat), 21 g protein, 41 g carbohydrate, 30 mg cholesterol, 1145 mg sodium, 7 g fiber

# PISTACHIO ICE CREAM

*Enjoy this fresh and summery treat on any warm and sunny day.*

**½ teaspoon whole cardamom**

**5 cups whole milk**

**Pinch saffron threads, crushed**

**1 (14-oz.) can sweetened condensed milk**

**1 cup whipping cream**

**¼ cup sugar**

**¼ cup chopped pistachios**

▶ Place cardamom in tea strainer or tie in cheesecloth; place in large saucepan. Add 4 cups of the milk and the saffron. Bring to a boil over medium heat, stirring constantly to prevent milk from scorching on bottom of saucepan.

▶ Boil milk over medium-low to medium heat about 45 minutes or until reduced by half, adjusting heat if necessary to keep a constant boil and stirring occasionally to make sure skin that forms on milk and sides of saucepan is stirred into mixture. This makes the ice cream buttery and rich.

▶ When milk is reduced to 2 cups, add remaining 1 cup milk, sweetened condensed milk, whipping cream and sugar. Return to a boil. Reduce heat to low; simmer 15 minutes, stirring occasionally.

▶ Remove and discard cardamom. (Mixture will contain milk particles, but do not strain.) Pour into large shallow pan; refrigerate until cool. Stir in pistachios.

▶ Freeze in ice cream maker according to manufacturer's instructions. Or place in large shallow pan. Place pan in freezer 2 hours. Then stir every ½ hour or until mixture thickens, for a total of 3 hours. Place in covered container; freeze overnight or until firm.

**8 (½)-cup servings**
PER SERVING: 385 calories, 20.5 g total fat (12 g saturated fat), 10.5 g protein, 42 g carbohydrate, 70 mg cholesterol, 150 mg sodium, .5 g fiber

## PEELING PISTACHIOS

Pistachios have a beautiful green color underneath their skin. To reveal that color, however, you have to peel off the skin. Here's an easy technique: bring a small pot of water to a boil. Add shelled pistachios and boil them 1 to 2 minutes or until the skins are softened. Drain the pistachios and place them on a clean towel. Then rub the nuts with the towel until their skin pops off.

# Suppers that Sizzle

## *Great fast food from your own skillet or grill.*

## GRILLED PORK CHOPS WITH CUBAN MOJO SAUCE

*Garlic—lots of it—is the key to this sauce's fabulous flavor, so make sure your garlic is very fresh. The sauce also would be a fine topper for other grilled meats, chicken, fish or vegetables.*

¾ teaspoon cumin seeds

4 large garlic cloves, coarsely chopped

1 jalapeño chile, veins and seeds removed, diced

2 tablespoons extra-virgin olive oil

½ teaspoon kosher (coarse) salt, divided

¼ teaspoon freshly ground pepper, divided

3 tablespoons lime juice

3 tablespoons orange juice

1 green onion, finely chopped

3 tablespoons chopped cilantro

2 bone-in pork rib chops (¾ to 1 inch thick)

▶ Heat grill. Place cumin seeds in mini food processor; pulse until coarsely cracked. Add garlic and chile; pulse until finely chopped. (Mixture also can be made by hand using a knife or mortar and pestle.)

▶ Heat oil in medium skillet over medium heat until warm. Add garlic mixture, ¼ teaspoon of the salt and ⅛ teaspoon of the pepper; cook 30 to 60 seconds or until garlic is fragrant but not browned. Stir in lime juice and orange juice. Remove from heat; stir in green onion and cilantro.

▶ Sprinkle pork chops with remaining ¼ teaspoon salt and ⅛ teaspoon pepper. Place chops on gas grill over medium-high heat or on charcoal grill 4 to 6 inches from medium-high coals; cover grill. Grill 6 to 8 minutes or until chops are pale pink in center, turning once.

▶ Place chops on plate; cover loosely with foil. Let stand 5 minutes. Spoon some sauce over each chop; serve remaining sauce for dipping.

**BEER/WINE** Try a dark beer, such as Negra Modelo from Mexico, or a Zinfandel wine.

**2 servings**
PER SERVING: 320 calories, 22 g total fat (4.5 g saturated fat), 24 g protein, 7 g carbohydrate, 65 mg cholesterol, 440 mg sodium, 1 g fiber

# SPINACH SALAD WITH GRILLED PORK TENDERLOIN AND STRAWBERRY VINAIGRETTE

*This salad's light, fresh vinaigrette lacks the overpowering sugariness of many purchased strawberry vinaigrettes. Make it when berries are plentiful.*

**VINAIGRETTE**

½ cup sliced strawberries

1½ teaspoons water

1½ teaspoons extra-virgin olive oil

½ teaspoon red wine vinegar

¼ teaspoon Dijon mustard

⅛ teaspoon freshly ground pepper

Dash salt

1 teaspoon finely chopped chives

**PORK**

1 (¾-lb.) pork tenderloin

⅛ teaspoon salt

⅛ teaspoon freshly ground pepper

**SALAD**

2 cups baby spinach

½ cup sliced strawberries

½ ripe avocado, thinly sliced

▶ Heat grill. Place all vinaigrette ingredients except chives in blender; blend until smooth. Stir in chives.

▶ Sprinkle pork with ⅛ teaspoon salt and ⅛ teaspoon pepper. Oil grill grate. Place pork on gas grill over medium heat or on charcoal grill 4 to 6 inches from medium coals; cover grill. Grill 10 to 12 minutes or until internal temperature reaches 145°F., turning once. Place on platter; cover loosely with foil. Let stand 5 minutes.

▶ Divide spinach between 2 plates; top with ½ cup strawberries. Drizzle each salad with 2 tablespoons of the vinaigrette. Slice pork diagonally; place on top of salads. Drizzle with additional vinaigrette; garnish with avocado.

**WINE** The acid in a vinaigrette poses a challenge in choosing a wine. Try a sparkling wine, or a lighter red, such as Pinot Noir.

**2 servings**
PER SERVING: 355 calories, 17 g total fat (4 g saturated fat), 40.5 g protein, 10.5 g carbohydrate, 110 mg cholesterol, 405 mg sodium, 5.5 g fiber

# SAUTÉED SHRIMP AND PASTA WITH SUGAR SNAP PEAS

*This recipe celebrates the colorful market vegetables of summer. Choose a pasta that will trap and hold all of the seasonings, such as farfalle, penne or fusilli.*

4 oz. farfalle (bow-tie pasta) (about 1½ cups)

¾ cup sugar snap peas

2½ tablespoons extra-virgin olive oil, divided

¼ teaspoon salt, divided

1 cup sliced onion

1 red bell pepper, thinly sliced

8 oz. shelled, deveined uncooked medium shrimp,
  tails removed

⅛ teaspoon freshly ground pepper

1 teaspoon grated lemon peel

½ teaspoon fennel seeds

½ teaspoon minced garlic

3 tablespoons thinly sliced fresh basil

¼ cup (1 oz.) crumbled feta cheese

▶ Cook farfalle in large pot of boiling salted water according to package directions. Add peas during last 1 minute of cooking; cook until bright green and crisp-tender. Drain. Return farfalle and peas to pot; sprinkle with ½ teaspoon of the oil and ⅛ teaspoon of the salt. Toss to combine.

▶ Meanwhile, heat large nonstick skillet over medium-high heat until hot. Add remaining 2 tablespoons oil; heat until hot. Add onion and bell pepper; cook 2 to 3 minutes or until slightly softened, stirring frequently. Reduce heat to medium.

▶ Sprinkle shrimp with remaining ⅛ teaspoon salt and pepper. Add to skillet, along with lemon peel, fennel seeds and garlic; cook 2 minutes or until shrimp just turn pink, stirring frequently to prevent garlic from browning. Stir in farfalle, peas and basil; toss until hot. Serve sprinkled with cheese.

**WINE** Choose a dry white, such as Sauvignon Blanc or Pinot Grigio.

**2 servings**
PER SERVING: 540 calories, 22 g total fat (5 g saturated fat), 29 g protein, 55 g carbohydrate, 175 mg cholesterol, 865 mg sodium, 6.5 g fiber

---

## GRILLING FOR TWO

The average charcoal fire requires about 40 briquettes, but you can use fewer coals when grilling for two. The key is to have a fire that lasts long enough, so you don't want to skimp.

Try using 25 to 30 pieces, concentrating them on one side of the grill. The fire should extend at least 2 inches beyond the food you're cooking.

# TURKEY BURGERS WITH MINT-YOGURT SAUCE

*Our testers were unanimous: These are the best turkey burgers they've ever tasted. The moist, juicy patties are topped off with a tangy mint-yogurt sauce. Ground turkey that contains some thigh meat (93 percent lean) is a more flavorful option for burgers than super-lean ground breast meat.*

### SAUCE

½ cup plain yogurt

1 garlic clove, minced

1 tablespoon extra-virgin olive oil

2 teaspoons lemon juice

½ teaspoon dried mint or 2 teaspoons finely chopped fresh mint

⅛ teaspoon salt

Dash freshly ground pepper

### BURGERS

1 garlic clove, minced

1 tablespoon minced green onion

1½ teaspoons Worcestershire sauce

1½ teaspoons Dijon mustard

1 teaspoon dried thyme or poultry seasoning

¼ teaspoon salt

⅛ teaspoon freshly ground black pepper

Dash cayenne pepper

8 oz. ground turkey

2 hamburger buns, split, toasted

▶ In small bowl, stir together all sauce ingredients. (Sauce can be made up to 3 hours ahead. Cover and refrigerate.)

▶ In medium bowl, stir together 1 garlic clove, green onion, Worcestershire sauce, mustard, thyme, ¼ teaspoon salt, ⅛ teaspoon black pepper and cayenne pepper. Gently stir in turkey just until blended (do not overmix).

▶ Form into 2 (3½-inch) patties ¾ inch thick. Heat grill pan or medium skillet over medium-high heat until hot; brush lightly with oil. Cook burgers 10 to 12 minutes or until no longer pink in center, turning once.* Serve burgers on buns; pass sauce separately.

**TIP** *Or place burgers on gas grill over medium-high heat or on charcoal grill 4 to 6 inches from medium-high coals; cover grill. Grill 10 to 12 minutes or until no longer pink in center, turning once.

**WINE** Choose a light, spicy red, such as Shiraz.

**2 sandwiches**
PER SANDWICH: 440 calories, 22 g total fat (5.5 g saturated fat), 30.5 g protein, 29.5 g carbohydrate, 80 mg cholesterol, 930 mg sodium, 1.5 g fiber

# BLUEBERRY CORNMEAL GEMS WITH GINGER WHIPPED CREAM

*Gems, popular in 19th century America, were miniature muffins that baked in special "gem" pans. Our version bakes in a muffin pan to create individual biscuits that are a bit smaller than the usual shortcake.*

**BLUEBERRIES**

4 cups blueberries

⅓ cup sugar

¼ cup crème de cassis liqueur or cranberry-raspberry juice

**GEMS**

1 cup all-purpose flour

1 cup cake flour

½ cup yellow cornmeal

¼ cup plus 1 teaspoon sugar

3½ teaspoons baking powder

1 teaspoon salt

1 teaspoon cream of tartar

¾ teaspoon ground cardamom

½ teaspoon baking soda

10 tablespoons unsalted butter, chilled, cut up

1 cup buttermilk

½ teaspoon vanilla

**CREAM**

2 cups whipping cream

¼ cup minced crystallized ginger

▶ In large bowl, combine blueberries, ⅓ cup sugar and liqueur; toss to mix. Mash slightly with potato masher or fork. Cover; refrigerate 1 hour.

▶ Meanwhile, heat oven to 350°F. Spray 12 muffin cups with nonstick cooking spray. In another large bowl, combine all-purpose flour, cake flour, cornmeal, ¼ cup of the sugar, baking powder, salt, cream of tartar, cardamom and baking soda; mix well.

▶ Add butter. Using pastry blender or 2 knives, cut in butter until mixture resembles coarse crumbs with pea-size pieces of butter. Add buttermilk and vanilla. Stir until dough forms.

▶ Spoon dough into muffin cups. Sprinkle with remaining 1 teaspoon sugar.

▶ Bake 25 to 30 minutes or until firm to the touch and tops are light brown. Remove from muffin cups; place on wire racks. Cool at least 15 minutes before serving.

▶ Meanwhile, in large bowl, whip cream at high speed until soft peaks form. Gently fold in ginger until evenly distributed. Cover; refrigerate until serving time.

▶ To serve, cut gems in half horizontally. Place bottom halves on individual dessert plates. Top with blueberries and their juices. Cover with top halves. Spoon cream over top. Refrigerate leftovers.

**12 servings**
PER SERVING: 395 calories, 23 g total fat (14 g saturated fat), 4.5 g protein, 43.5 g carbohydrate, 70 mg cholesterol, 435 mg sodium, 2.5 g fiber

*Casual recipes that rely on fast, easy methods.*

# WARM CHICKEN SALAD WITH FRESH PEACHES

*This arranged salad, drizzled with a honey mustard vinaigrette, makes a lovely presentation for a casual summer supper. Watch the pine nuts while they're toasting; they can overbrown quickly.*

### SALAD

2 boneless skinless chicken breast halves

1 teaspoon olive oil

1 teaspoon lemon-pepper seasoning

4 cups mixed salad greens

1 peach, thinly sliced

2 tablespoons toasted pine nuts

1 oz. (¼ cup) shaved Parmesan or Romano cheese

### VINAIGRETTE

2¼ teaspoons white wine vinegar

½ teaspoon honey mustard

⅛ teaspoon minced garlic

⅛ teaspoon freshly ground pepper

Dash salt

2 tablespoons olive oil

▶ Heat broiler or grill. Brush chicken with 1 teaspoon olive oil; sprinkle with lemon-pepper seasoning. Broil 4 to 6 inches from heat, or grill on gas grill over medium heat or on charcoal grill 4 to 6 inches from medium coals. Cook 8 to 10 minutes or until no longer pink in center, turning once. Let stand 3 minutes; thinly slice.

▶ Meanwhile, in small bowl, whisk together all vinaigrette ingredients except oil. Slowly whisk in 2 tablespoons oil until combined.

▶ In large bowl, toss greens with vinaigrette; place on platter. Top with sliced chicken, peach slices, pine nuts and cheese.

**WINE**  A young Chardonnay, with its fruit flavors, is ideal here.

**2 servings**
PER SERVING: 425 calories, 28 g total fat (6.5 g saturated fat), 34.5 g protein, 10 g carbohydrate, 75 mg cholesterol, 665 mg sodium, 3 g fiber

# STIR-FRIED ORANGE PORK

*When slicing the pork for this Chinese-inspired entree, make sure the strips are thin so that they'll cook quickly. Serve the dish over white or brown rice, or over wilted mustard greens, for a traditional presentation.*

1½ tablespoons peanut oil

3 tablespoons matchstick-sized pieces orange peel*

4 dried Chinese red chiles or ¼ teaspoon crushed
  red pepper**

1 garlic clove, slivered

8 oz. center-cut boneless pork chops, sliced (⅛ inch)

2 cups broccoli florets

½ cup reduced-sodium chicken broth

¼ cup orange juice

1 tablespoon soy sauce

1 tablespoon dry sherry

1 tablespoon sugar

1 tablespoon cornstarch

1 tablespoon water

▶ Heat wok or large skillet over medium heat until hot. Add oil; heat until hot. Add orange peel, chiles and garlic. Cook 3 minutes, stirring frequently.

▶ Increase heat to high; add pork. Cook 1 to 2 minutes or just until pork loses raw pink color. Stir in broccoli; cook 1 minute.

▶ Stir in broth, orange juice, soy sauce, sherry and sugar; cover and cook 1 minute.

▶ Meanwhile, in small bowl, whisk together cornstarch and water; stir into sauce. Cook 30 to 60 seconds or until thickened, stirring constantly. Remove and discard chiles before serving.

TIPS *Use vegetable peeler to cut thin strips of orange peel; slice strips into matchstick-sized pieces.

**Dried Chinese red chiles are common in Szechuan and Hunan cooking. Look for bright red whole chiles, not dull or torn ones. They are often available in bulk at Asian markets.

WINE This dish pairs well with either a white or a red wine. Try Chardonnay or Pinot Noir.

**2 servings**
PER SERVING: 375 calories, 19.5 g total fat (5 g saturated fat), 28.5 g protein, 21.5 g carbohydrate, 70 mg cholesterol, 700 mg sodium, 2.5 g fiber

# MU SHU VEGETABLE WRAPS

*Peanut sauce and aromatic vegetables are combined and folded inside a flour tortilla for a no-fuss meal.*

### SAUCE

2 tablespoons creamy peanut butter

1½ tablespoons soy sauce

1½ tablespoons water

2 teaspoons rice vinegar

1 teaspoon sugar

¼ teaspoon freshly ground pepper

### WRAPS

2 tablespoons peanut oil

2 green onions, thinly sliced

1 garlic clove, minced

2 teaspoons minced fresh ginger

2 cups thinly sliced cabbage

2 cups broccoli florets

2 cups thinly sliced portobello mushroom caps

4 (8-inch) flour tortillas

▶ In small bowl, whisk all sauce ingredients until well combined.

▶ Heat oil in wok or large skillet over medium heat until hot. Add green onions, garlic and ginger; cook 30 seconds, stirring constantly.

▶ Add cabbage, broccoli and mushrooms; cook 1 minute. Pour in peanut butter sauce. Cover pan; reduce heat to low. Cook 4 minutes or until vegetables are crisp-tender. Spoon mixture into flour tortillas; roll up.

**WINE**  The spice in this dish calls for a delicate but not-too-dry white wine, such as Pinot Grigio.

**2 servings**
PER SERVING: 575 calories, 28.5 g total fat (5 g saturated fat), 17.5 g protein, 67.5 g carbohydrate, 0 mg cholesterol, 1290 mg sodium, 9 g fiber

## DESSERTS FOR DUOS

### Grilled Caramel Pineapple

Once the grilling is done and the grill is still hot, don't forget dessert. Pineapple slices turn even sweeter when grilled. Lightly oil the grill; grill 4 (½-inch-thick) pineapple slices over medium-high heat for 4 minutes or until they're softened and marked with golden stripes, turning once. Place 2 slices on each plate; top each with 2 tablespoons of purchased caramel topping and 1 teaspoon of toasted chopped hazelnuts.

### Chocolate-Covered Berries

Late summer and early fall is the time for plump, sweet blackberries or raspberries. They're even better when covered with a decadent chocolate sauce. In a small saucepan, heat 1½ oz. of semisweet chocolate, 3 tablespoons of heavy whipping cream and a dash of cinnamon over very low heat for 1 to 3 minutes, stirring constantly, or just until the chocolate is melted. Remove the pan from the heat; stir in 2 teaspoons of Cointreau, Grand Marnier or orange juice. Divide 1 cup of berries between 2 shallow bowls; pour the sauce over the berries.

# SHRIMP AND ARTICHOKE FRITTATA

*This dish is similar to an omelet but easier to make because you don't have to flip it. Cooking the frittata over low heat helps it firm up, allowing you to easily cut it into two portions.*

5 eggs

2 tablespoons milk

1 tablespoon olive oil

1 garlic clove, minced

⅓ lb. shelled, deveined uncooked medium shrimp

¼ teaspoon salt

¼ teaspoon freshly ground pepper

1 (6-oz.) jar marinated artichoke hearts, drained, chopped

▶ In medium bowl, whisk together eggs and milk.

▶ Heat oil in medium (8-inch) ovenproof nonstick skillet over medium heat until hot. Add garlic; cook 10 to 20 seconds or until fragrant. Add shrimp; cook 1 minute, stirring frequently. Sprinkle with salt and pepper. Pour in egg mixture; cook 30 to 60 seconds or until edges begin to set. Sprinkle top with artichoke hearts. Cover; reduce heat to low. Cook 8 to 10 minutes or until almost set.

▶ Meanwhile, heat broiler. Remove cover; broil frittata 4 to 6 inches from heat 2 to 3 minutes or until lightly browned. Run heatproof spatula around edges to loosen frittata from skillet.

**WINE** The earthiness of the shrimp and artichokes calls for a dry, earthy white. Try Sauvignon Blanc or Pinot Grigio.

**2 servings**
PER SERVING: 370 calories, 22.5 g total fat (5.5 g saturated fat), 30.5 g protein, 12 g carbohydrate, 640 mg cholesterol, 840 mg sodium, 4.5 g fiber

# LIME CHEESECAKE WITH FRESH FRUIT

*A careful combination of lower-fat ingredients produces a lighter cheesecake with creamy texture and wonderfully satisfying flavor. The fresh fruit topping is an ideal partner for the bright lime taste of the filling.*

### CHEESECAKE

2 (8-oz.) pkg. reduced-fat cream cheese, softened

1 (8-oz.) pkg. fat-free cream cheese, softened

1 (14-oz.) can fat-free sweetened condensed milk

1 egg

3 egg whites

3 tablespoons all-purpose flour

2 tablespoons fresh lime juice

2 teaspoons grated lime peel

### TOPPING

3 cups assorted fresh berries

1 kiwi fruit, halved, sliced

1 nectarine, cut into thin wedges

½ cup red currant jelly, melted

▶ Heat oven to 325°F. Wrap foil around outside of 9-inch springform pan to prevent leaks while baking.

▶ In large bowl, beat reduced-fat and fat-free cream cheese and condensed milk on medium speed until smooth and creamy. Add egg and egg whites; beat until smooth. Add flour, lime juice and lime peel; beat until well mixed. Pour into springform pan.

▶ Place springform pan in large, shallow roasting pan or broiler pan. Fill large pan with enough hot water to come halfway up sides of springform pan.

▶ Bake 45 to 50 minutes or until edges are puffed and top looks dull and is dry to the touch. Remove from oven; let stand in water bath 30 minutes. Remove from water bath; cool completely on wire rack. Refrigerate at least 4 hours; cover and store in refrigerator up to 3 days.

▶ Up to 3 hours before serving, arrange fruit over cheesecake. Brush melted jelly over fruit. Refrigerate until glaze is set.

**12 servings**
PER SERVING: 280 calories, 10 g total fat (4.5 g saturated fat), 40 mg cholesterol, 390 mg sodium, 2 g fiber

# THAI BEEF SALAD

*Marinating this steak has two benefits: It makes the meat extra tender and flavorful, and the juices from the steak give depth to the dressing. An essential ingredient is fish sauce, which can be found in Asian groceries and some supermarkets. While it looks like light-colored soy sauce, it has a pronounced fishy aroma. But don't let your nose fool you; the delicate, not-very-fishy taste is incomparable.*

6 oz. boneless beef top sirloin steak (½ inch thick)

2 tablespoons lime juice

2 tablespoons fish sauce

1½ tablespoons peanut oil

1½ teaspoons sugar

⅛ to ¼ teaspoon crushed red pepper

2 cups baby spinach, watercress or mixed salad greens

4 radishes, thinly sliced

½ cucumber, thinly sliced

¼ cup coarsely chopped fresh mint

¼ cup coarsely chopped fresh cilantro

¼ cup thinly sliced halved sweet onion

▶ Heat grill. Oil grill grate. Place steak on gas grill over medium-high heat or on charcoal grill 4 to 6 inches from medium-high coals; cover grill. Grill 4 minutes for medium-rare or until of desired doneness, turning once. Let stand 10 minutes; thinly slice across grain.

▶ In large bowl, stir together lime juice, fish sauce, oil, sugar and crushed red pepper. Add sliced steak; stir to coat. Refrigerate up to 20 minutes, turning occasionally.

▶ Add spinach, radishes, cucumber, mint, cilantro and onion to steak mixture; toss gently to coat.

**WINE** Select a spicy, not-too-heavy red to serve with this salad.

**2 (3-cup) servings**
PER SERVING: 235 calories, 13 g total fat (2.5 g saturated fat), 19.5 g protein, 10 g carbohydrate, 45 mg cholesterol, 595 mg sodium, 2 g fiber

# CHICKEN SALTIMBOCCA

*This recipe is the reverse of a stuffed chicken breast; the sage is placed on top of the chicken and secured with a slice of prosciutto that's wrapped around the breast. Saltimbocca is traditionally made with veal; this version uses chicken breasts.*

2 boneless skinless chicken breast halves
4 large or 6 medium fresh sage leaves
6 slices very thinly sliced prosciutto
  (about 3 oz.)
2 teaspoons olive oil
¼ cup reduced-sodium chicken broth
1 tablespoon lemon juice

▶ Place chicken breasts between 2 sheets of plastic wrap; with flat side of meat mallet, pound to flatten chicken slightly. Place 2 or 3 sage leaves on top of each breast. Place 3 slices prosciutto over sage on each chicken breast. Wrap prosciutto around chicken; secure with toothpick, if necessary.

▶ Heat oil in medium nonstick skillet over medium-high heat until hot. Add chicken, sage side down; cook 8 minutes or until browned and no longer pink in center, turning once. Place on heatproof plate.

▶ Return skillet to heat; add broth. Boil 1½ minutes or until broth is reduced to about 1 tablespoon, stirring to scrape up any browned bits from bottom of skillet. Return chicken and any accumulated juices to skillet. Add lemon juice; boil until sauce thickens and glazes chicken, turning chicken occasionally. Remove toothpicks before serving.

**WINE** Serve a white that's richly flavored but not heavy. Try a lighter Chardonnay or a slightly earthy Sauvignon Blanc.

**2 servings**
PER SERVING: 275 calories, 14 g total fat (3.5 g saturated fat), 34.5 g protein, 1 g carbohydrate, 95 mg cholesterol, 460 mg sodium, 0 g fiber

---

## SUMMER SALAD FOR TWO

Garden vegetables dominate in this take-off of a Middle Eastern bread salad, called fattoush. Serve it alongside grilled meats.

### Middle Eastern Pita Salad

Tear 1 large pita bread into bite-sized pieces; lightly toast in oven. In large bowl, stir together 1½ cups chopped tomato, 1½ cups chopped cucumber, ¼ cup chopped fresh parsley, 2 tablespoons chopped fresh cilantro, 2 tablespoons chopped fresh mint, 2 chopped green onions and ⅛ teaspoon minced garlic. Add toasted pita bread. Drizzle salad with 2 tablespoons lemon juice and 2 tablespoons extra-virgin olive oil. Sprinkle with dash of salt; toss well.

# GRILLED SHRIMP WRAPS

*The creaminess of the avocado ties together all the flavors and textures in these simple, fresh-tasting wraps. If you use wooden or bamboo skewers, leave enough time to soak them in water for at least 30 minutes before grilling. Also, don't let the shrimp marinate for more than 20 minutes or they'll start to "cook" in the lime juice, ceviche-style.*

6 tablespoons lime juice

2 large garlic cloves, minced

¼ to ½ teaspoon crushed red pepper

¼ plus ⅛ teaspoon salt, divided

12 oz. shelled, deveined uncooked medium shrimp

1 avocado, chopped

⅓ cup sour cream

1 tablespoon chopped fresh cilantro

1½ cups mixed salad greens

4 (8-inch) flour tortillas

6 radishes, thinly sliced

▶ If using wooden skewers, soak 6 (6- to 8-inch) skewers in enough water to cover 30 minutes.

▶ Heat grill. In medium bowl, stir together lime juice, garlic, crushed red pepper and ⅛ teaspoon of the salt. Reserve 2 tablespoons of the marinade. Add shrimp to remaining marinade; stir to coat. Refrigerate 15 to 20 minutes, stirring occasionally.

▶ Meanwhile, in small bowl, mash avocado with fork. Stir in sour cream, cilantro, 1 tablespoon of the reserved marinade and remaining ¼ teaspoon salt. In another medium bowl, toss greens with remaining 1 tablespoon reserved marinade.

▶ Remove shrimp from marinade; pat dry. Discard marinade. Thread shrimp onto skewers.* Place skewers on gas grill over medium-high heat or on charcoal grill 4 to 6 inches from medium-high coals; cover grill. Grill 2 minutes or until shrimp turn pink, turning once. Place on plate; cover to keep warm.

▶ Place tortillas between sheets of damp paper towel. Microwave on high 10 to 15 seconds or just until softened.

▶ To serve, spread each tortilla with one-fourth of the avocado mixture. Top with one-fourth of the shrimp, greens and radishes. Roll or fold up.

**TIP** *Shrimp also can be placed directly on grill grate.

**BEER/WINE** Try either a slightly spicy beer, such as Dos Equis from Mexico, or Pinot Gris.

**4 wraps**
PER WRAP: 315 calories, 14 g total fat (4.5 g saturated fat), 18.5 g protein, 29.5 g carbohydrate, 135 mg cholesterol, 545 mg sodium, 4 g fiber

# CORNMEAL-CRUSTED SCALLOPS WITH CORN RELISH

*The sweet flavor and delicate texture of sea scallops make them an ideal pairing with the sweet-and-sour corn relish. When corn season is over, you can prepare the relish with 1½ cups thawed frozen corn, although it won't be as crunchy.*

1 small red bell pepper, diced (¼ inch)

½ medium onion, diced (¼ inch)

¼ cup cider vinegar

1 tablespoon sugar

¾ teaspoon salt, divided

¼ teaspoon celery seeds

⅛ teaspoon mustard seeds

1½ cups corn kernels (from 2 medium ears corn)

2 tablespoons all-purpose flour

2 tablespoons cornmeal

12 oz. jumbo sea scallops

¼ teaspoon freshly ground pepper

1 tablespoon olive oil

▶ Place bell pepper, onion, vinegar, sugar, ½ teaspoon of the salt, celery seeds and mustard seeds in large skillet. Bring to a simmer over medium heat; cook 5 minutes or until pepper is slightly softened and liquid has almost evaporated, stirring frequently. Stir in corn; cook and stir 3 minutes or until corn is crisp-tender. Cool to room temperature.

▶ In small shallow plate, stir together flour and cornmeal. Sprinkle scallops with remaining ¼ teaspoon salt and pepper; toss scallops in flour mixture to coat. Heat medium skillet over medium-high heat until hot. Add oil; heat until hot. Add scallops; cook 3 to 4 minutes or until light brown and center is barely opaque, turning once. Serve scallops with corn relish.

**WINE** Scallops are perfect with a Sauvignon Blanc.

**2 servings**
PER SERVING: 330 calories, 9 g total fat (1 g saturated fat), 23.5 g protein, 43.5 g carbohydrate, 25 mg cholesterol, 1120 mg sodium, 4.5 g fiber

# VIOLET BERRY FOOL

*A fool is an old-fashioned English dessert in which pureed berries are folded into whipped cream.*

**4 cups blackberries\***
**1½ cups blueberries**
**¾ cup sugar**
**1 cup whipping cream**
**3 tablespoons sugar**
**2 tablespoons blackberry-flavored brandy**
  **or orange-flavored liqueur, if desired**
**Edible flowers (Johnny jump-ups, violets**
  **or pink dianthus), if desired**

▶ In food processor or blender, puree blackberries. Press pureed mixture through strainer to remove seeds; discard seeds. In medium bowl, combine blackberry puree, blueberries and ¾ cup sugar; toss gently to mix.

▶ In another medium bowl, beat cream, 3 tablespoons sugar and brandy until stiff peaks form. Gently fold cream mixture into berry mixture. Do not overmix; streaked berry mixture should give a marbled look to the cream.

▶ Spoon into individual dessert dishes or parfait glasses. Garnish with edible flowers. Serve immediately.

**TIP** \*Berries and whipping cream can be prepared ahead; store in separate containers in refrigerator. When ready to serve, fold mixtures together as directed above.

**4 servings**
PER SERVING: 460 calories, 19 g total fat (11.5 g saturated fat), 65 mg cholesterol, 25 mg sodium, 0 g fiber

## BERRY GUIDE
### Blackberries

These more or less oblong berries look like overgrown black raspberries, with a distinguishing difference: When you pick a raspberry, the core remains on the bush and you're left with a berry that has a hollow center. When you pick a blackberry, the edible core remains in the berry. As with black raspberries, look for fruit that is black-purple all over; avoid fruit that is still tinged with pink or white.

### Blueberries

Tiny, wild blueberries are generally more intensely flavored than the large cultivated varieties commonly found in the market, but either may be used in recipes. Look for berries that are evenly blue (with a slightly dusty-looking whitish haze over the blue skin) without patches of white or green or pink, which indicate immaturity. Rinse just before using.

# PORK CHOPS WITH PEACHES AND BASIL

*Peaches and fresh basil add a taste of summer to moist, tender pork chops. The juices in which the peaches are cooked are wonderfully savory, thanks to the addition of sherry vinegar. Be sure to peel and cut the peaches before starting to cook the pork.*

½ teaspoon salt

½ teaspoon paprika

¼ teaspoon freshly ground pepper

2 boneless pork loin chops (1 inch thick)

1 tablespoon vegetable oil

¼ cup minced shallots

2 tablespoons sherry vinegar or red wine vinegar

2 peaches, peeled, each cut into 8 wedges*

¼ cup reduced-sodium chicken broth or water

2 tablespoons chopped fresh basil

▶ In small bowl, stir together salt, paprika and pepper. Sprinkle over both sides of pork chops.

▶ Heat oil in heavy large skillet over medium-high heat until hot. Add pork; cook 8 to 10 minutes or until browned and pale pink in center, turning once. Place on plate; cover loosely with foil.

▶ Add shallots to same skillet; cook and stir over medium heat 1 minute. Add vinegar; stir to scrape up any browned bits from bottom of skillet. Add peaches and broth; cook 2 minutes, mashing a few peach slices with fork. Spoon peaches over pork; sprinkle with basil.

**TIP** *To peel peaches, drop peaches into large pot of boiling water; boil 30 seconds or until peach skins loosen. Remove with slotted spoon; drop into ice water to cool. Use knife to peel away skin.

**WINE** A fruit-forward, medium-bodied red such as Pinot Noir brings together all the flavors of this dish.

**2 servings**
PER SERVING: 285 calories, 15 g total fat (4 g saturated fat), 24.5 g protein, 14 g carbohydrate, 65 mg cholesterol, 700 mg sodium, 3.5 g fiber

# SAUSAGE AND PEPPERS IN SPANISH RICE

*Sweet and smoky flavors blend seamlessly in this satisfying weeknight meal. Many supermarkets now carry precooked flavored sausages; look for brands such as Emeril's, Al Fresco or Aidells. The chicken and sun-dried tomato sausages have a great taste. For more heat, use a spicy sausage.*

2 precooked flavored chicken sausage links (6 to 8 oz. total)

1 tablespoon olive oil

1 medium red bell pepper, cut into ¾-inch pieces

1 small onion, chopped

2 large garlic cloves, minced

1 (14.5-oz.) can diced tomatoes

1½ cups water

½ cup long-grain rice

½ teaspoon salt

½ teaspoon smoked or regular paprika*

¼ teaspoon saffron threads, crushed

1 cup frozen peas

▶ Heat grill. Place sausages on gas grill over medium-high heat or on charcoal grill 4 to 6 inches from medium-high coals; cover grill. Grill 5 to 8 minutes or until browned, turning occasionally.** Slice ½ inch thick.

▶ Meanwhile, heat oil in Dutch oven over medium heat until hot. Add bell pepper, onion and garlic; cook 6 minutes or until vegetables are tender, stirring frequently. Stir in tomatoes, water, rice, salt, paprika and saffron. Bring to a boil, stirring occasionally. Reduce heat to low; cover and simmer 15 minutes or until rice is almost tender.

▶ Stir in sausage and peas; cook, covered, 3 to 5 minutes or until rice is fully cooked.

**TIPS** *Smoked paprika comes in mild and hot versions and adds a pleasant smoky taste to foods. It can be found in markets carrying foods from Spain or online at www.tienda.com. Chipotle powder can be substituted for smoked paprika, but it will add a spicy bite.

**Sausages also can be cooked in grill pan over medium-high heat 5 minutes or until browned, turning occasionally.

**WINE** A light, spicy red is a nice pick.

**2 (2-cup) servings**
PER SERVING: 525 calories, 17.5 g total fat (4 g saturated fat), 24 g protein, 68 g carbohydrate, 50 mg cholesterol, 1470 mg sodium, 7 g fiber

# CHICKEN WITH SPICY FRESH TOMATO SAUCE

*Because tomatoes are the centerpiece of this dish and cook for just 2 minutes, make sure to use ripe, juicy ones. The sauce gets a bit of heat from red pepper.*

**3 medium tomatoes, seeded, chopped**

**2 tablespoons chopped fresh Italian parsley**

**1½ tablespoons olive oil, divided**

**1 large garlic clove, minced**

**½ teaspoon salt**

**¼ teaspoon freshly ground black pepper**

**⅛ teaspoon crushed red pepper**

**2 boneless skinless chicken breast halves**

▶ In medium bowl, stir together tomatoes, parsley, 1 tablespoon of the oil, garlic, salt, black pepper and crushed red pepper.

▶ Heat remaining ½ tablespoon oil in medium skillet over medium-high heat until hot. Add chicken; cook 6 minutes or until browned and no longer pink in center, turning once. Place on plate; cover loosely with foil.

▶ Add tomato mixture to same skillet; cook and stir 2 minutes. Spoon sauce over chicken.

**WINE** Try a Chianti with fresh fruit and light spice with this chicken.

**2 servings**
PER SERVING: 280 calories, 14.5 g total fat (2.5 g saturated fat), 28.5 g protein, 9.5 g carbohydrate, 75 mg cholesterol, 675 mg sodium, 2 g fiber

---

## ONE VEGETABLE SERVES TWO

### Parmesan-Crusted Tomatoes

Halve 1 large tomato; sprinkle cut sides with salt and pepper. Generously sprinkle chopped fresh herbs, such as basil, mint and/or chives, over tomatoes. Top with freshly grated Parmesan cheese. Broil tomatoes until cheese is melted and tomatoes are warm.

### Lemon-Dill Zucchini

Halve 1 medium zucchini; slice. Melt 1 tablespoon butter in medium skillet. Cook 1 minced garlic clove in butter until fragrant. Add zucchini; cook 2 to 3 minutes or until crisp-tender. Toss with 2 teaspoons lemon juice and 2 teaspoons chopped fresh dill.

### Twice-Baked Cheddar Melts

Microwave 1 large russet potato until tender. Halve lengthwise; scoop out pulp. Mix with 1/4 cup low-fat sour cream, salt and pepper. Scoop mixture into potato shells; top with shredded cheddar cheese. Bake or microwave potatoes until cheese is melted and potatoes are hot.

# TUNA, WHITE BEAN AND TOMATO SALAD

*This tasty salad requires very little chopping, so it goes together quickly. The onions are combined with the vinegar first to subdue the raw onion bite.*

¼ medium red onion, thinly sliced

2 tablespoons red wine vinegar

¼ teaspoon sugar

¼ teaspoon salt

3 cups mixed salad greens

1 (15-oz.) can navy beans, drained, rinsed

1 (6-oz.) can tuna packed in oil or water,
   drained, flaked

⅔ cup halved grape or cherry tomatoes

1 tablespoon extra-virgin olive oil

2 tablespoons chopped fresh herbs, such as
   parsley, basil and/or mint

⅛ teaspoon freshly ground pepper

▶ In small bowl, stir together onion, vinegar, sugar and salt.

▶ Place greens on platter. Top with beans, tuna, tomatoes and onion mixture. Drizzle with oil; sprinkle with herbs and pepper.

**WINE** A dry, earthy Sauvignon Blanc pairs wonderfully with this salad.

**2 (2-cup) servings**
PER SERVING: 470 calories, 15 g total fat (2.5 g saturated fat), 39.5 g protein, 46.5 g carbohydrate, 15 mg cholesterol, 1180 mg sodium, 12 g fiber

# CARAMEL APPLE BREAD PUDDING

*Sautéed sliced apples bathed in a rich caramel syrup are the perfect complement to this outstanding pudding.*

## PUDDING

1 tablespoon butter

3 medium, tart apples (such as Braeburn or Fuji), peeled, cut into ½-inch pieces (3 cups)

½ cup coarsely chopped toasted pecans

1½ cups milk

1 cup whipping cream

30 caramels

3 eggs

¼ cup packed brown sugar

1 teaspoon cinnamon

¼ teaspoon salt

1 tablespoon vanilla

5 cups loosely packed, cubed (1½ inch) stale French bread

## TOPPING

½ cup butter

2 large Fuji, Braeburn or Golden Delicious apples, unpeeled, sliced

½ cup packed brown sugar

▶ In large heavy skillet, melt 1 tablespoon butter. Add cut-up apples; cook over medium heat, turning frequently, until apples are lightly browned and thoroughly cooked. Set aside.

▶ Lightly butter 9x5x3-inch (2-quart) loaf pan. Sprinkle pecans over bottom of pan. In medium saucepan, heat milk and cream over medium heat until very hot but not boiling. Add caramels; cook and stir until melted.

▶ Heat oven to 350°F. In large bowl, whisk together eggs, ¼ cup brown sugar, cinnamon, salt and vanilla. Slowly whisk in hot caramel mixture. Add bread cubes and cooked apples; let stand 30 minutes.

▶ Spoon mixture into loaf pan. Bake 50 to 60 minutes or until set but still slightly soft in center. Cool completely on wire rack.

▶ Melt ½ cup butter in skillet over medium heat. Add sliced apples; cook until apples are tender but not mushy. Stir in ½ cup brown sugar; cook and stir until apples are coated.

▶ Unmold pudding onto plate; cut into thick slices. Place on individual dessert plates. Spoon warm apple slices and sauce over each serving.

**10 servings**
PER SERVING: 475 calories, 26.5 g total fat (14 g saturated fat), 6.5 g protein, 55 g carbohydrate, 125 mg cholesterol, 310 mg sodium, 2.5 g fiber

# FALL
# & WINT

# TER
# cooking

# Spice is Nice

*From pepper to pesto, spices add zip to weeknight meals.*

## HUEVOS RANCHEROS TOSTADAS

*Sometimes the best thing for dinner is breakfast. This filling dish gets a touch of spiciness from the chile and a satisfying crunch from the tostada shells. You can make your own shells by frying 5-inch corn tortillas until crisp with just a little corn oil or canola oil.*

4 eggs

2 tablespoons milk

1 small jalapeño chile, veins and seeds removed, finely chopped

½ teaspoon salt

¼ teaspoon freshly ground pepper

1 tablespoon unsalted butter

3 tablespoons chopped cilantro, divided

4 (5-inch) tostada shells

6 tablespoons (1½ oz.) shredded Monterey Jack cheese

½ cup refrigerated salsa

1 small avocado, diced

▶ Heat broiler. In small bowl, whisk together eggs, milk, chile, salt and pepper. Melt butter in medium skillet over medium heat. Add eggs; cook 2 minutes or until softly scrambled, stirring frequently. Stir in 2 tablespoons of the cilantro.

▶ Place tostada shells on small baking sheet. Divide scrambled eggs among shells; top with cheese. Broil 4 to 6 inches from heat 30 to 60 seconds or just until cheese is melted and bubbly.

▶ Sprinkle tostadas with remaining 1 tablespoon cilantro; serve with salsa and avocado.

**BEER/WINE** Pair this dish with a Mexican beer, such as Dos Equis Amber, or a light, slightly spicy red wine.

**2 servings**
PER SERVING: 515 calories, 36 g total fat (13 g saturated fat), 23 g protein, 28 g carbohydrate, 460 mg cholesterol, 1180 mg sodium, 7.5 g fiber

# PENNE WITH SAUSAGE AND BROCCOLI RAAB

*To add a touch of heat to this pasta, use hot Italian sausage in place of the sweet variety. If it comes in links, squeeze out the sausage meat and break it into clumps in the skillet.*

4 oz. penne (tube-shaped pasta)

2 teaspoons olive oil

4 oz. bulk sweet or hot Italian sausage

½ small onion, chopped

2½ cups coarsely chopped broccoli raab
   (about 3 oz.)*

¼ cup white wine or chicken broth

1 cup Italian-seasoned diced canned tomatoes

1 tablespoon prepared basil pesto

2 tablespoons freshly grated Parmesan cheese

▶ Cook penne in large pot of boiling salted water according to package directions; drain.

▶ Meanwhile, heat oil in medium skillet over medium-high heat until hot. Add sausage and onion; cook 4 to 5 minutes or until sausage just loses its pink color and onion is softened, stirring frequently. Stir in broccoli raab and wine. Cover; reduce heat to medium. Cook 3 to 5 minutes or until broccoli raab is just tender. Uncover; stir in tomatoes and pesto. Cook 3 minutes or until broccoli raab is tender, stirring frequently.

▶ Toss penne with sausage mixture; sprinkle with cheese.

**TIP** *Broccoli raab, also known as rapini or rape, has long stalks with tiny broccoli-like buds. Its slightly bitter taste is very popular in Italy, where it's used in salads, pastas, soups and other preparations. Look for it in the produce section of the supermarket.

**WINE** This pasta dish works best with a dry Pinot Gris.

**2 (1¾-cup) servings**
PER SERVING: 510 calories, 22.5 g total fat (6.5 g saturated fat), 21.5 g protein, 55 g carbohydrate, 40 mg cholesterol, 975 mg sodium, 6.5 g fiber

# BUTTERMILK PAN-FRIED CHICKEN

*Buttermilk, cornmeal and thyme create a delicious crust on these tender chicken breasts. In addition to providing a lemony tang, buttermilk helps keep the chicken juicy.*

2 boneless skinless chicken breast halves

½ cup buttermilk, divided

3 tablespoons cornmeal

3 tablespoons all-purpose flour, divided

1½ teaspoons chopped fresh thyme, divided

½ teaspoon plus ⅛ teaspoon salt, divided

½ teaspoon freshly ground pepper

2 tablespoons canola oil

½ cup reduced-sodium chicken broth

▶ With flat side of meat mallet, flatten chicken to ½ inch; place in small shallow dish. Pour ¼ cup of the buttermilk over chicken; turn to coat both sides. Let stand 10 minutes at room temperature.

▶ In another small shallow dish, stir together cornmeal, 2 tablespoons of the flour, ¾ teaspoon of the thyme, ½ teaspoon of the salt and pepper. Dip chicken in cornmeal mixture to coat completely.

▶ Heat oil in medium skillet over medium-high heat until hot. Add chicken; cook 6 to 8 minutes or until golden brown and no longer pink in center, turning once. Place on plate.

▶ Whisk remaining 1 tablespoon flour into drippings in skillet. Cook and stir 2 minutes or until paste is golden brown. Whisk in broth, remaining ¾ teaspoon thyme and ⅛ teaspoon salt. Cook, scraping up any browned bits from bottom of skillet, until sauce comes to a boil. Boil 1 minute. Whisk in remaining ¼ cup buttermilk; reduce heat to medium-low. Cook and stir 1 minute or until hot (do not boil). Serve chicken with sauce.

**WINE**  Try Pinot Grigio, a dry and delicate choice.

**2 servings**
PER SERVING: 360 calories, 18 g total fat (2.5 g saturated fat), 31 g protein, 16.5 g carbohydrate, 75 mg cholesterol, 800 mg sodium, 1 g fiber

## SAVING LEFTOVER INGREDIENTS

Left with a partial can of chicken broth or tomato sauce? Here are some ways to store and use leftover ingredients :

### Buttermilk

Store in the refrigerator up to 2 weeks; use what remains in homemade biscuits, pancakes and smoothies.

### Canned Stock or Broth

Store in a plastic container and refrigerate up to

3 days or freeze in 1/2-cup amounts up to 6 months. Purchase broth in resealable boxes for handy refrigerator storage.

### Fresh Herbs

Lightly wrap in paper towels, place in an opened plastic bag and store in the refrigerator. Chop and toss in salads over the next few days, or chop and freeze in resealable plastic bags.

# SMOKED PORK CHOPS WITH SPICED RAISIN CHUTNEY

*Sweet meets smoky in this quick-to-fix main course. Look for smoked pork chops in the fresh meat or bacon section of the grocery store.*

¼ cup raisins

⅓ cup apple juice

2 smoked pork chops (6 oz. boneless or about
    10 oz. bone-in)

¼ teaspoon salt, divided

¼ teaspoon freshly ground pepper, divided

1 tablespoon unsalted butter, divided

3 tablespoons finely chopped onion

½ cup diced apple

Dash ground cloves

4 teaspoons cider vinegar

2 teaspoons chopped fresh sage

▶ Place raisins and apple juice in small bowl; let stand 15 minutes.

▶ Meanwhile, sprinkle both sides of pork chops with ⅛ teaspoon of the salt and ⅛ teaspoon of the pepper. Melt ½ tablespoon of the butter in medium skillet over medium-high heat. Add pork chops; cook 4 to 6 minutes or until golden brown, turning once. Place on plate.

▶ Melt remaining ½ tablespoon butter in same skillet over medium heat. Add onion; cook 1 to 2 minutes or until just softened, stirring frequently. Stir in apple, cloves and vinegar, scraping up any browned bits from bottom of skillet. Add raisins with apple juice, sage, remaining ⅛ teaspoon salt and remaining ⅛ teaspoon pepper. Reduce heat to medium-low; simmer 2 to 3 minutes to blend flavors, stirring frequently.

▶ Return pork chops to skillet; cover and simmer 2 to 3 minutes or until pork chops are heated through. Serve topped with chutney.

**2 servings**
PER SERVING: 285 calories, 13 g total fat (6 g saturated fat), 18 g protein, 26 g carbohydrate, 60 mg cholesterol, 1425 mg sodium, 1.5 g fiber

# ORANGE GINGERBREAD WITH CITRUS CREAM

*This traditional gingerbread is accented with orange peel and a double hit of ginger—crystallized and ground. The orange-infused cream topping is a heavenly complement.*

**GINGERBREAD**

½ cup butter, softened

½ cup sugar

1 cup molasses

2 eggs

2 teaspoons grated orange peel

2½ cups all-purpose flour

2 tablespoons chopped crystallized ginger

1 teaspoon baking soda

½ teaspoon salt

2 teaspoons cinnamon

1½ teaspoons ground ginger

½ teaspoon ground cloves

1 cup buttermilk

**CITRUS CREAM**

1½ cups whipping cream

2 tablespoons sugar

¼ cup orange marmalade

2 tablespoons orange juice

2 teaspoons grated orange peel

▶ Heat oven to 350°F. Grease 13x9x2-inch pan. In large bowl, beat butter at medium speed until fluffy. Slowly add ½ cup sugar; beat 2 to 3 minutes until light and creamy. Add molasses; mix well. Add eggs and 2 teaspoons orange peel; mix until well blended.

▶ In medium bowl, combine flour, crystallized ginger, baking soda, salt, cinnamon, ground ginger and cloves; mix well. Alternately add flour mixture and buttermilk to butter mixture, beating just until combined. Pour batter into pan. Bake 35 to 40 minutes or until toothpick inserted in center comes out clean. Cool 15 to 30 minutes. Meanwhile, in large bowl, combine cream and 2 tablespoons sugar; beat at high speed until slightly thickened. Add marmalade, orange juice and 2 teaspoons orange peel; beat until soft peaks form. Refrigerate until ready to serve. Serve gingerbread warm with Citrus Cream.

**15 servings**
PER SERVING: 320 calories, 14.5 g total fat (9 g saturated fat), 4.5 g protein, 44 g carbohydrate, 75 mg cholesterol, 250 mg sodium, 1 g fiber

# COCONUT-CURRY CHICKEN AND POTATOES

*With this dish's vibrant flavors, no one will guess it gets much of its creamy richness from soymilk. When choosing a brand to cook with, be sure to read labels; many are loaded with sugars that would turn the curry into dessert. The brand we used had only 4 grams of sugar and 5 grams of fat per serving.*

1 large (10-oz.) russet potato, peeled, cut into 1-inch pieces

1 tablespoon canola oil

1 boneless skinless chicken breast half, cut into 1-inch pieces

½ medium onion, chopped

1 tablespoon chopped jalapeño chile

2 teaspoons minced fresh ginger

2 teaspoons curry powder

¾ cup plain soymilk

½ cup unsweetened coconut milk*

1 cup halved grape or cherry tomatoes

¼ teaspoon salt

2 tablespoons chopped fresh cilantro

▶ Place potato in medium saucepan; add enough cold water to cover. Bring to a boil; cook 10 to 15 minutes or until barely tender. Drain.

▶ Meanwhile, heat oil in large nonstick skillet over medium-high heat until hot. Add chicken; cook 3 minutes or until browned and no longer pink in center, turning occasionally. Place on plate.

▶ Add onion, jalapeño and ginger to same skillet. Cook, stirring occasionally, 3 minutes or until onion is translucent. Stir in curry powder; cook an additional 30 seconds or until fragrant.

▶ Add potato, chicken with any accumulated juices, soymilk, coconut milk, tomatoes and salt. Bring to a boil; cook, stirring occasionally, 5 minutes or until thickened. (Curry will be slightly soupy. If desired, thicken sauce by breaking up about one-fourth of the potato pieces with spoon as you stir.) Sprinkle with cilantro.

**TIP** *If desired, freeze remaining coconut milk from can for another use.

**2 (1¾-cup) servings**
PER SERVING: 430 calories, 24 g total fat (12.5 g saturated fat), 20.5 g protein, 38 g carbohydrate, 35 mg cholesterol, 355 mg sodium, 6 g fiber

# LAMB PATTIES WITH YOGURT SAUCE

*These lamb patties get a healthy boost from flax seeds. The finely ground seeds help keep the patties soft, and they thicken the sauce, too.*

6 oz. ground lamb

4 tablespoons minced onion, divided

1 egg, separated

2 tablespoons finely ground flax seeds

1 garlic clove, minced

¼ teaspoon ground cumin

½ cup nonfat plain yogurt

Dash salt

2 teaspoons olive oil

¼ cup reduced-sodium chicken broth

2 tablespoons chopped fresh mint

▶ In medium bowl, combine lamb, 2 tablespoons of the onion, egg white, flax seeds, garlic and cumin until well blended; let stand 5 minutes or until slightly firm (mixture will be soft). Shape into 2 (4½-inch) patties.

▶ Meanwhile, in small bowl, whisk together egg yolk, yogurt and salt until smooth.

▶ In small nonstick skillet, heat oil over medium-high heat until hot. Add patties; cook 5 to 7 minutes or until no longer pink in center, turning once. Place on plate.

▶ Add remaining 2 tablespoons onion to skillet. Cook over medium to medium-low heat, stirring frequently, 2 to 3 minutes or until softened. Add broth. Increase heat to medium-high; cook, stirring occasionally, 3 to 4 minutes or until broth has evaporated. Stir in yogurt mixture; cook and stir 1 to 2 minutes or until bubbling. Pour over patties; sprinkle with mint.

**2 servings**
PER SERVING: 265 calories, 14.5 g total fat (3.5 g saturated fat), 24 g protein, 9.5 g carbohydrate, 155 mg cholesterol, 320 mg sodium, 2 g fiber

# PASTA WITH TOMATOES AND CANNELLINI BEANS

*This dish is Italian peasant fare at its best. The cheese sprinkled on at the end brings all the flavors together, so be sure to use the good stuff—real Parmesan cheese, imported from Italy. The sauce may seem thin at first, but it thickens as it sits.*

1 tablespoon olive oil

½ small onion, finely chopped

½ small carrot, finely chopped

½ rib celery, finely chopped

1 garlic clove, minced

½ teaspoon fennel seeds, crushed

1 (14½-oz.) can diced tomatoes, undrained

1 (14-oz.) can reduced-sodium chicken or vegetable broth

1 (15-oz.) can cannellini beans, drained, rinsed

4 oz. small pasta (such as ditalini or small shells)

2 cups lightly packed chopped escarole or Swiss chard

¼ cup (1 oz.) freshly grated Parmigiano-Reggiano cheese

▶ In large nonstick skillet, heat oil over medium-high heat until hot. Add onion, carrot and celery; cook 2½ minutes or until vegetables begin to soften. Add garlic and fennel seeds; cook 30 seconds or until fragrant.

▶ Add tomatoes and broth; bring to a boil. Reduce heat to low; simmer 5 minutes or until vegetables are soft.

▶ Increase heat to medium. Add beans and pasta. Bring to a simmer; cook, stirring occasionally, 10 to 15 minutes or until pasta is just tender. Stir in escarole; cook 2 to 4 minutes or until wilted. Serve in wide soup bowls; sprinkle with cheese.

**WINE** This classic Tuscan pasta calls for a Chianti Classico.

**2 (2-cup) servings**
PER SERVING: 630 calories, 14 g total fat (4 g saturated fat), 31.5 g protein, 96.5 g carbohydrate, 10 mg cholesterol, 1335 mg sodium, 18.5 g fiber

# MISO-GLAZED SALMON

*Marinating fish in sweet white miso (fermented soybean paste) is a classic Japanese technique that works brilliantly with a rich fish such as salmon. The salty-sweet miso flavors the fish and turns to a shiny glaze as the fish cooks. Put together this easy dish the night before so it has time to marinate. Serve it with roasted asparagus topped with sesame seeds.*

½ cup sweet white miso*
¼ cup medium-dry sherry**
1 tablespoon packed dark brown sugar
2 (6-oz.) salmon fillets, skin removed
2 teaspoons canola oil

▶ In small bowl, stir together miso, sherry and brown sugar until smooth. Spread ⅓ cup of the mixture in bottom of small glass or ceramic baking dish. Place salmon on top; spread with remaining mixture to coat completely. Cover with plastic wrap; refrigerate at least 12 hours or up to 24 hours.

▶ When ready to cook, heat broiler; oil small broiler pan. Remove salmon from marinade; discard marinade. Pat salmon dry with paper towels. Place in pan; drizzle with oil. Cook 4 to 6 inches from heat 3 to 5 minutes or until salmon just begins to flake.

**TIPS** *Miso, a slightly sweet and salty fermented soybean paste, is at the heart of traditional Japanese cooking. The lighter colored varieties are used in delicate soups and sauces, while the darker colored versions appear in heavier dishes. You'll find miso in the refrigerated section of supermarkets or at Asian markets or health food stores. It can be stored in the refrigerator up to 3 months.

**For a nonalcoholic version of the marinade, substitute an equal amount of alcohol-free beer for the sherry. Increase the brown sugar to 2 tablespoons and add a teaspoon of sherry vinegar or rice vinegar.

**WINE** Try a soft, fruity red that picks up on the various flavors in this dish.

**2 servings**
PER SERVING: 410 calories, 18.5 g total fat (4 g saturated fat), 50 g protein, 7.5 g carbohydrate, 150 mg cholesterol, 760 mg sodium, 1 g fiber

# CLASSIC CRÈME BRULÉE

*This is the classic crème brulée, perfect in its simplicity. For best flavor, take the time to find vanilla beans — the result is worth the extra step. If not using the vanilla bean, choose a high quality vanilla extract.*

> 4 cups whipping cream
> ½ cup sugar
> ½ vanilla bean or 2 teaspoons vanilla extract
> 8 egg yolks
> ⅓ cup packed light brown sugar

▶ Heat oven to 300°F. Place 8 (½- to ¾-cup) ramekins in shallow roasting pan.

▶ In large saucepan, combine cream and sugar. If using vanilla bean, cut in half lengthwise; scrape out vanilla seeds. Add scraped pod and seeds to cream mixture. (If using vanilla extract, add in step 3.) Heat mixture until small bubbles form around edge of pan. Remove saucepan from heat; cover and let steep 10 minutes.

▶ Place egg yolks in large bowl; whisk until blended. Add cream mixture slowly to egg yolks, whisking constantly. If using vanilla extract, stir into custard. Strain mixture through fine strainer. Pour custard into ramekins. Add enough boiling water to roasting pan to reach halfway up sides of ramekins. Cover pan securely with foil.

▶ Bake 50 to 60 minutes or until custard is set but still quivery like gelatin.

▶ With tongs, remove ramekins from hot water; cool on wire rack 30 to 40 minutes or until room temperature. Cover ramekins with plastic wrap; refrigerate at least 1 hour or up to 24 hours.

▶ Place oven rack 8 inches from broiler; heat broiler. Push brown sugar through strainer over each custard, allowing about 2 teaspoons per custard. Using fingers, gently spread brown sugar to distribute evenly. Place ramekins in shallow roasting pan; surround ramekins with ice cubes.

▶ Broil 8 inches from heat for 3 to 6 minutes or until brown sugar melts and caramelizes, watching carefully to prevent burning. Cool to room temperature. Store in refrigerator. (If made more than 4 hours ahead, topping will begin to soften and will no longer be crisp.)

**8 servings**
PER SERVING: 495 calories, 42 g total fat (24.5 g saturated fat), 345 mg cholesterol, 50 mg sodium, 0 g fiber

## HERB-BRINED TURKEY BREAST WITH BOURBON PAN GRAVY

*Brining is an ideal method for turkey because it adds flavor and moisture. It's especially easy to do with a turkey breast. You'll have leftovers with this recipe—perfect for sandwiches the next day.*

**TURKEY**

⅓ cup sea or kosher (coarse) salt

¼ cup packed light brown sugar

1 cup mixed fresh herb sprigs (such as sage, thyme, marjoram and parsley), divided

4 whole cloves

4 whole allspice

4 whole peppercorns

2 to 3 cups water, divided

1 bone-in turkey breast half (2½ to 3 lb.)

1 tablespoon unsalted butter, softened

½ teaspoon freshly ground pepper

**GRAVY**

1 tablespoon all-purpose flour

1⅓ cups reduced-sodium chicken broth

2 tablespoons bourbon whiskey or additional chicken broth

▶ Place salt, brown sugar, ⅓ cup of the herb sprigs, cloves, allspice, peppercorns and 1 cup of the water in heavy-duty resealable plastic freezer bag; stir to dissolve salt and sugar. Place turkey in bag; add enough additional water to barely cover turkey. Seal bag; turn several times to coat turkey with brine. Refrigerate at least 2 hours or up to 6 hours, turning frequently. Remove turkey from brine; discard brine. Rinse turkey well; pat dry.

▶ Heat oven to 350°F. Chop enough of the remaining mixed herbs to measure 2 tablespoons, reserving 1 tablespoon of the chopped herbs for gravy and several sprigs for garnish. In small bowl, blend remaining 1 tablespoon chopped herbs into butter. With fingers, loosen turkey skin from meat; rub butter under skin, spreading as much as possible over breast. Place turkey, skin side up, on rack in small roasting pan; sprinkle with pepper. Bake 1 hour 10 minutes to 1 hour 20 minutes or until internal temperature reaches 170°F. Place turkey breast on platter; loosely cover. Let stand 15 to 20 minutes.

▶ Meanwhile, spoon off all but about 1 tablespoon of the fat from pan drippings. Place roasting pan over medium heat. Whisk in flour; cook 2 minutes or until flour is lightly browned. Slowly whisk in broth until gravy is smooth. Bring to a boil; cook 3 to 5 minutes or until slightly thickened. Stir

in reserved 1 tablespoon chopped herbs and bourbon. Simmer 2 minutes.
To serve, slice turkey breast; serve on bed of reserved herb sprigs. Serve with gravy.

**4 servings**
PER SERVING: 550 calories, 26 g total fat (8.5 g saturated fat), 69.5 g protein, 4 g carbohydrate, 195 mg cholesterol, 1100 mg sodium, 0 g fiber

# BACON AND CORNBREAD DRESSING

*Cornbread and bacon give this moist, fluffy dressing its fabulous sweet-and-smoky flavor. Red bell pepper adds beautiful flecks of color.*

3 slices thick-cut bacon

2 tablespoons unsalted butter

1 small onion, chopped

1 rib celery, chopped

1 small red bell pepper, chopped

1 teaspoon freshly ground pepper

2 cups cubed day-old cornbread or corn muffins
(about 8 oz.)

2 to 4 tablespoons reduced-sodium chicken broth

▶ Heat oven to 350°F. Cook bacon in medium skillet over medium heat until crisp. Drain; coarsely crumble. (If making dressing ahead, cover and refrigerate bacon until ready to bake.) Pour off all but 1 tablespoon drippings from skillet. Add butter; cook until melted. Add onion, celery and bell pepper; cook over medium heat, stirring frequently, 3 to 5 minutes or until vegetables are softened. Sprinkle with pepper. Add cornbread and 2 tablespoons broth; toss to mix well. If dressing seems dry, add remaining 2 tablespoons broth. (Stuffing can be made to this point up to 1 day ahead. Cover and refrigerate.)

▶ Stir in crumbled bacon. Spread in shallow 2-quart baking dish or 9-inch deep-dish pie plate. Bake, uncovered, 20 to 30 minutes or until hot and crusty on top.

**2 servings**
PER SERVING: 625 calories, 40 g total fat (18.5 g saturated fat), 15 g protein, 51.5 g carbohydrate, 135 mg cholesterol, 1240 mg sodium, 4 g fiber

## WINES FOR THE THANKSGIVING MEAL

Choosing wine for Thanksgiving may seem challenging, but it needn't be. let the food take center stage and choose wines that won't compete with the dishes – full bodied fruity or spicy white wines and lighter red wines usually work best. Here are a few suggestions:

### Beaujolais

Fruity, refreshing Beaujolais is possibly the best of all wines to accompany Thanksgiving.

### Chardonnay

Look for clean, fruity Chardonnays. Steer clear of those that are over-oaked or too buttery.

### Riesling and Gewürztraminer

The best of these lively, spicy white wines come from Alsace.

### Viognier

Once you try Viognier, with its tropical fruit and spice flavors, it may replace Chardonnay as your favorite white wine.

### Dessert Wines and Tawny Port

The deep apricot and nut flavors found in late-harvest Gewürztraminers and Rieslings pair deliciously with pumpkin pie and other Thanksgiving desserts. Another excellent, surprising choice is 10- to 20-year-old tawny port.

# GINGERED CRANBERRY-KUMQUAT RELISH

*This intensely colorful relish is the perfect accompaniment for roast turkey. Its sweet-tart taste is enhanced by the bright bite of ginger.*

**1 cup fresh cranberries**

**3 kumquats, quartered***

**¼ cup sugar**

**1 tablespoon chopped crystallized ginger**

▶ Place cranberries, kumquats, sugar and ginger in food processor; pulse until finely chopped. Place in small bowl; refrigerate at least 2 hours or overnight.

**TIP** *If kumquats are unavailable, substitute ¼ cup chopped orange.

**WINE** Turkey works well with either a white or red wine that isn't too full-bodied. For white, try Pinot Blanc, a wine that's drier and lighter than Chardonnay. For red, select Pinot Noir.

¾ **cup**
PER 2 TABLESPOONS: 50 calories, 0 g total fat (0 g saturated fat), 0 g protein, 13.5 g carbohydrate, 0 mg cholesterol, 5 mg sodium, 1.5 g fiber

---

## KUMQUATS AT A GLACE

### Season

Late November through June

### Varieties

The main types of kumquats available in the United States are Meiwa and Nagami. They can be used interchangeably in recipes.

### Sources

Kumquats can be found at most supermarkets and Asian markets.

### Choosing and Storing

Look for firm fruit with glossy skin. Kumquats that are soft will be less juicy, but they are perfectly acceptable for most uses. Store them in a plastic bag in the vegetable drawer of the refrigerator for up to three weeks.

### Preparation Tips

To remove seeds, slice kumquats in half and squeeze them gently; the seeds will pop out. Seeds also can be removed after thinly slicing the kumquats. Blanching whole kumquats for 20 to 30 seconds in boiling water before slicing or chopping them will soften them just enough to be added to stuffings, cakes and muffins. Seeded kumquats can be pureed and used as a flavoring and thickening agent in sauces, dressings, cakes, creams and frostings.

### Nutrition

One kumquat has about 12 calories and is a good source of vitamin C.

# TWICE-BAKED POTATOES WITH HERBS

*For potato lovers, this dish delivers the best of both worlds—buttery mashed potatoes and crunchy potato skins. To save time, the potatoes can be baked, mashed and stuffed back into the shells a day ahead.*

2 medium baking potatoes

¼ cup half-and-half or whole milk

1 tablespoon unsalted butter, softened

1 tablespoon chopped fresh parsley

1 tablespoon chopped fresh chives or green onions

¼ teaspoon salt

¼ teaspoon freshly ground pepper

3 tablespoons shredded sharp cheddar cheese

▶ Heat oven to 350°F.

▶ Prick potatoes in several places with fork; place on oven rack. Bake 1 hour or until tender. Remove from oven; let stand 20 minutes or until cool enough to handle. Cut a thin lengthwise slice off tops of potatoes; scoop out insides. Place in medium bowl, leaving potato skins and ¼ inch of flesh as shells.

▶ Add half-and-half and butter; mash until nearly smooth (small lumps are fine). Stir in parsley, chives, salt and pepper. Spoon potato mixture evenly into skins. (Potatoes can be made to this point up to 1 day ahead. Cover and refrigerate. Baking time may need to be increased by about 10 minutes.) Sprinkle with cheese.

▶ Place potatoes in baking dish. Bake 15 to 20 minutes or until cheese is melted and potatoes are hot.

**2 servings**
PER SERVING: 270 calories, 13 g total fat (8 g saturated fat), 6.5 g protein, 32.5 g carbohydrate, 40 mg cholesterol, 380 mg sodium, 3 g fiber

---

## CLEANING HERBS

Sturdy herbs and some packaged herbs require just a thorough rinse under cold water and patting dry with a paper towel. But large bunches of parsley, basil, cilantro and dill may harbor grit, so wash them carefully as you would your salad greens. Strip leaves from stems. Place leaves in a salad spinner basket and set it in the basin of a salad spinner. (Or use a colander set in a large bowl.) Fill the basket with cold water and swish. Let soak for a few minutes, then lift out the basket. Repeat the process until no trace of grit remains in the basin. Spin herbs dry. It is important to dry herbs thoroughly before storing or chopping.

---

# PECAN TARTS

*Individual tarts make a pretty presentation, and it's fun to have your very own. You can easily double this recipe and bake it in four individual tart pans, if you wish. Serve the tarts with sweetened whipped cream or ice cream.*

**1 (15-oz.) refrigerated pie crust**

**2 tablespoons dark corn syrup**

**2 tablespoons packed dark brown sugar**

**2 tablespoons beaten egg\***

**½ tablespoon unsalted butter, melted**

**¼ teaspoon vanilla extract**

**½ cup coarsely chopped pecans**

▶ Unfold pie crust; cut 2 (5-inch) circles from crust. Ease each circle into 4-inch round tart pan with removable bottom, pressing against edges and folding under any overhang. Place tart shells on small baking sheet; freeze 10 minutes.

▶ Heat oven to 400°F.

▶ In small bowl, whisk together corn syrup, brown sugar, egg, butter and vanilla until smooth. Divide pecans evenly between tart shells; pour filling over pecans. (Tart shells will be quite full.) Place on baking sheet.

▶ Place baking sheet with tarts in oven. Bake 20 to 25 minutes or until pastry is golden brown and filling is puffed and browned. Remove tarts from baking sheet; cool completely on wire rack. Serve at room temperature.

**TIP** *To measure egg, break 1 egg in small bowl; beat until smooth. Measure 2 tablespoons; discard remaining egg or reserve for another use.

**2 tarts**
PER TART: 600 calories, 39.5 g total fat (7.5 g saturated fat), 7.5 g protein, 59 g carbohydrate, 70 mg cholesterol, 405 mg sodium, 3 g fiber

## BAKED MUSTARD-APPLE CHICKEN BREASTS

*Leaving the chicken breasts on the bone adds extra flavor to this homey fall dish. The bones also work as a natural rack, raising the breasts off the bottom of the pan.*

4 teaspoons Dijon mustard

1 teaspoon packed light brown sugar

1 teaspoon canola oil

¼ teaspoon ground ginger

¼ teaspoon plus ⅛ teaspoon salt, divided

⅛ teaspoon freshly ground pepper

2 bone-in skinless chicken breast halves

1 tablespoon panko*

¼ teaspoon dried thyme

1 Gala apple, cut into 8 wedges

1 medium red onion, cut into 12 wedges

▶ Heat oven to 400°F. In small bowl, stir together mustard, brown sugar, oil, ginger, ¼ teaspoon of the salt and pepper; spread over chicken. In another small bowl, stir together panko, thyme and remaining ⅛ teaspoon salt; sprinkle evenly over chicken, pressing lightly to adhere.

▶ Spray bottom of small shallow roasting pan with nonstick cooking spray; arrange apple and onion over bottom of pan. Top with chicken.

▶ Bake 30 to 35 minutes or until chicken is no longer pink in center and juices run clear.

**TIP** *Panko are coarse bread crumbs usually found next to other bread crumbs in the supermarket.

**WINE** A crisp and light Pinot Grigio/Pinot Gris is a nice match here.

**2 servings**
PER SERVING: 385 calories, 10.5 g total fat (2.5 g saturated fat), 51.5 g protein, 20 g carbohydrate, 135 mg cholesterol, 830 mg sodium, 3 g fiber

# CHEDDAR AND PORTOBELLO MUSHROOM SKILLET

*Casual and comforting, this smoky, mushroom-intensive vegetarian offering cuts preparation time by using packaged shredded cheddar cheese and hash brown potatoes. The mushrooms provide a satisfying heartiness.*

1 tablespoon olive oil

1 small onion, chopped

1 medium carrot, chopped

1 rib celery, chopped

1½ teaspoons minced garlic

1 (6-oz.) pkg. portobello mushrooms, diced

1 large tomato, diced

¼ teaspoon salt

⅛ teaspoon freshly ground pepper

⅛ teaspoon dried rosemary, crushed

2 cups frozen shredded potatoes (hash browns)

½ cup (2 oz.) shredded cheddar cheese

▶ Heat oil in medium skillet over medium heat until hot. Add onion, carrot and celery; cook 4 to 5 minutes or until onion softens, stirring occasionally. Add garlic; cook 30 to 60 seconds or until fragrant. Stir in mushrooms, tomato, salt, pepper and rosemary.

▶ Reduce heat to medium-low; cook an additional 10 minutes or until mushrooms have released their juices and liquid is reduced and thickened. Top with potatoes; reduce heat to low. Cover and cook 8 minutes. Top with cheese; cook 2 minutes or until cheese is melted.

**WINE** Try a light red, such as Merlot.

**2 servings**
PER SERVING: 425 calories, 17 g total fat (7 g saturated fat), 15 g protein, 56.5 g carbohydrate, 30 mg cholesterol, 560 mg sodium, 8.5 g fiber

# MOROCCAN LAMB CHOPS

*Serve these tender chops with a side of couscous and a simple salad of tomatoes and cucumbers dressed with lemon juice, olive oil and chopped fresh mint.*

**2 tablespoons lemon juice**

**2 tablespoons olive oil**

**1 tablespoon chopped fresh mint**

**1 tablespoon chopped fresh cilantro**

**1½ teaspoons minced garlic**

**1 teaspoon ground cumin**

**½ teaspoon ground cinnamon**

**¼ teaspoon ground ginger**

**¼ teaspoon salt**

**Dash cayenne pepper**

**4 lamb loin chops (about 1 lb.)**

▶ Combine lemon juice, olive oil, mint, cilantro, garlic, cumin, cinnamon, ginger, salt and pepper in resealable plastic bag; squeeze bag to blend ingredients. Add lamb; seal bag. Turn several times to coat lamb. Let stand 15 to 20 minutes, turning once.

▶ Meanwhile, heat broiler. Remove lamb from marinade; discard marinade. Broil lamb 4 to 6 inches from heat 6 to 10 minutes for medium-rare or until of desired doneness, turning once.

**WINE** Syrah has light, spicy flavors that work well with the lamb.

**2 servings**
PER SERVING: 250 calories, 15 g total fat (4 g saturated fat), 26 g protein, 1.5 g carbohydrate, 85 mg cholesterol, 65 mg sodium, .5 g fiber

---

## SQUASH FOR TWO

Acorn squash is the perfect vegetable for two people. Here's an easy and delicious way to prepare it: Spray a foil-lined baking sheet with nonstick cooking spray. Halve and seed the squash. Place it on the baking sheet and bake it at 350°F., cut side down, for 45 to 50 minutes or until tender. Turn the squash over; sprinkle with salt and pepper, and boost the flavor with one of these toppings before serving.

### Browned Butter, Honey and Sage

Melt 2 tablespoons butter in small saucepan over medium-low heat until it turns medium brown, swirling occasionally to keep from burning. Add 2 tablespoons honey and ½ teaspoon dried sage. Drizzle over cavity of each squash.

### Maple-Bacon Topping

Cook 2 strips of bacon; drain and crumble. Brush inside of squash, including cavity, with 3 tablespoons maple syrup; sprinkle with crumbled bacon.

### Marmalade and Jalapeño

Remove veins and seeds from 1 jalapeño chile; finely chop. Heat 3 tablespoons of orange marmalade with chile in small saucepan until marmalade is melted. Spoon into cavity of each squash.

# APRICOT BALSAMIC GLAZED SALMON

*Apricot preserves and balsamic vinegar team up in an enticing and updated sweet-sour topping that's tasty and attractive.*

¼ cup apricot preserves

2 tablespoons balsamic vinegar

1 teaspoon minced ginger

¾ teaspoon minced garlic

⅛ teaspoon salt

2 (6-oz.) salmon fillets, skin removed

▶ Heat oven to 425°F.

▶ Line shallow baking pan with foil; spray with nonstick cooking spray.

▶ In small saucepan, heat preserves, vinegar, ginger, garlic and salt over low heat 3 to 4 minutes or until slightly thickened, stirring occasionally. Remove from heat; cool slightly.

▶ Place salmon fillets on baking sheet; top with apricot glaze. Bake 10 to 12 minutes or until salmon just begins to flake.

**WINE** A Pinot Noir is a delicious complement to the salmon.

**2 servings**
PER SERVING: 360 calories, 9.5 g total fat (3 g saturated fat), 36.5 g protein, 29.5 g carbohydrate, 110 mg cholesterol, 255 mg sodium, .5 g fiber

---

## CHOOSING SALMON

Five types of Salmon are typically found in markets:

### King or Chinook

The Largest, most flavorful and most coveted of the Pacific species, and also one of the most expensive. Flesh color ranges from creamy white to deep orange-red.

### Atlantic

The only salmon native to the Atlantic Ocean; it is sometimes labeled by the country or origin—Chile, Norway and Scotland. Its flesh is orange, and it has a rich flavor similar to king.

### Sockeye or Red

Rich red flesh, highly prized in Japan, where nearly all the Alaskan sockeye is sold. It ranks with king and Atlantic in flavor.

### Coho or Silver

Small coho, farmed in fresh water, is often featured on menus as a whole, stuffed "baby" salmon. It looks and tastes similar to trout.

### Chum or Silverbite

Pale pink to red flesh; the cheapest species of salmon. The chum catch is the last of the year, so fresh, wild salmon in the fall is likely this species.

# CHOCOLATE-ESPRESSO FUDGE PIE

*This filling is divine—moist, chewy and intensely chocolaty. Dress it up with vanilla-scented whipped cream.*

CRUST

**1 (9-inch) pie crust**

FILLING

**½ cup unsalted butter, cut up**

**2 oz. unsweetened chocolate, coarsely chopped**

**1 oz. semisweet chocolate, coarsely chopped**

**3 eggs**

**1⅓ cups sugar**

**3 tablespoons light corn syrup**

**2 tablespoons sour cream**

**1 tablespoon instant espresso powder**

**1 teaspoon vanilla**

TOPPING

**2 cups whipping cream**

**2 tablespoons sugar**

**1 teaspoon vanilla**

**Chocolate shavings for garnish**

▶ Position oven rack in lower third of oven; heat oven to 350°F. In small saucepan, combine butter, unsweetened chocolate and semisweet chocolate. Heat over low heat until melted. Set aside to cool.

▶ In medium bowl, combine all remaining filling ingredients; beat until well blended. Stir in melted chocolate mixture. Pour into pie crust.

▶ Bake on oven rack in lower third of oven 35 to 40 minutes or until filling puffs up but center is still slightly wobbly. (Some cracks may form around edge of pie.) Check pie after first 20 minutes of baking; if pie crust appears to be browning too quickly, cover edges with foil to protect crust. Cool on wire rack. Pie filling will sink as it cools.

▶ In large bowl, beat whipping cream on high speed until cream begins to slightly thicken. Add sugar and vanilla; beat until soft peaks form. Serve pie with whipped cream and chocolate shavings. Store in refrigerator.

**8 servings**
PER SERVING: 555 calories, 33 g total fat (18 g saturated fat), 6.5 g protein, 61.5 g carbohydrate, 165 mg cholesterol, 180 mg sodium, 2 g fiber

## SESAME-GARLIC SIRLOIN STEAK

*Broiled sirloin steak gets fabulous flavor from sesame seeds and a variety of Asian condiments; you can find them in the Asian section of the grocery store or in Asian markets. Dark sesame oil adds a rich, nutty sesame taste, while hoisin sauce contributes a bit of sweetness.*

**2 tablespoons soy sauce**

**2 tablespoons hoisin sauce**

**1 tablespoon dark sesame oil**

**1 teaspoon chili-garlic sauce**

**2 garlic cloves, minced**

**12 oz. boneless beef top sirloin steak (1 inch thick)**

**2 tablespoons chopped cilantro**

**1 teaspoon sesame seeds, toasted***

▶ In resealable plastic bag, combine soy sauce, hoisin sauce, sesame oil, chili-garlic sauce and garlic; add steak. Seal bag; turn to coat both sides. Refrigerate at least 30 minutes.

▶ Heat broiler; place steak on broiler pan. Reserve marinade. Spoon half of the reserved marinade over steak. Broil 4 to 6 inches from heat 8 to 10 minutes for medium-rare or until of desired doneness, turning once and brushing with marinade.

▶ Place steak on cutting board. Cover loosely with foil; let stand 5 minutes before slicing thinly. Sprinkle with cilantro and sesame seeds.

**TIP** *To toast sesame seeds, heat small dry skillet over medium heat. Add sesame seeds; shake skillet continuously until seeds are lightly browned, 1 to 2 minutes.

**WINE** Serve Shiraz to accompany this steak.

**2 servings**
PER SERVING: 280 calories, 10 g total fat (2.5 g saturated fat), 40 g protein, 5.5 g carbohydrate, 95 mg cholesterol, 655 mg sodium, .5 g fiber

# PAN-SEARED LAMB CHOPS WITH BALSAMIC GLAZE

*You'll be amazed at all the rich flavor you get from only six ingredients. Balsamic vinegar and brown sugar are combined with the browned bits in the skillet and reduced to form a sweet, glossy glaze that partners well with the tender lamb.*

**4 lamb loin chops (1 inch thick)
(about 1¼ lb.)**

**1 teaspoon dried rosemary**

**½ teaspoon salt**

**¼ teaspoon freshly ground pepper**

**2 tablespoons balsamic vinegar**

**1 tablespoon packed light brown sugar**

▶ Sprinkle lamb chops with rosemary, salt and pepper.

▶ Heat large nonstick skillet over medium-high heat until hot. Add lamb chops; cook 4 minutes. Reduce heat to low. Turn chops; cook an additional 3 to 4 minutes for medium-rare or until of desired doneness. Place on 2 plates.

▶ Add vinegar and brown sugar to skillet; bring to a boil over low heat. Cook 1 to 2 minutes or until slightly thickened, scraping up any browned bits from bottom of skillet. Pour glaze over chops.

**WINE** Try Cabernet Sauvignon, a rich wine at a great value.

**2 servings**
PER SERVING: 260 calories, 10.5 g total fat (3.5 g saturated fat), 32 g protein, 8 g carbohydrate, 105 mg cholesterol, 675 mg sodium, .5 g fiber

# RED CURRY PORK TENDERLOIN

*A simple blend of on-hand spices quickly jazzes up pork tenderloin. If you'd like a little more heat, increase the cayenne pepper to ¼ teaspoon or use Madras curry powder. Serve the pork with couscous and steamed green beans.*

1 teaspoon paprika
½ teaspoon curry powder
¼ teaspoon garlic salt
¼ teaspoon freshly ground black pepper

⅛ teaspoon cayenne pepper
2 teaspoons olive oil or garlic-flavored
   olive oil
1 (12-oz.) pork tenderloin

▶ Heat oven to 400°F. In small bowl, stir together paprika, curry powder, garlic salt, black pepper and cayenne pepper. Brush oil evenly over pork; sprinkle with spice mixture, patting to coat. Place on rack in shallow baking dish or on broiler pan.

▶ Bake 15 to 20 minutes or until internal temperature reaches 145°F. Place pork on cutting board. Cover loosely with foil; let stand 5 minutes before slicing.

**BEER/WINE** A flavorful dark beer such as Sierra Nevada Porter from California picks up on the spice in this dish. Or serve a red wine.

**2 servings**
PER SERVING: 255 calories, 11 g total fat (3 g saturated fat), 36.5 g protein, 65 g carbohydrate, 100 mg cholesterol, 195 mg sodium, .5 g fiber

---

## SHEDDING LIGHT ON DARK SESAME OIL

Aromatic, nutty-tasting dark sesame oil is a pantry staple for Asian cooking. It is a delightful enhancement to marinades (see Sesame-Garlic Sirloin Steak, pg. 120), noodle salads, dressings or dipping sauces.

• Dark sesame oil is produced by pressing toasted sesame seeds into oil. It's typically used as a seasoning that's added at the end of cooking to finish a dish, rather than as a cooking medium, because its distinctive flavor is lost when exposed to high heat. While dark sesame oil is often associated with stir-fries, it does not stand up well to the high temperatures used in this technique. Instead, it's better to use a more heat-tolerant, neutral-tasting oil like peanut oil for stir-frying, and then use dark sesame oil to flavor the sauce.

• Don't confuse dark sesame oil with light sesame oil, which is extracted from untoasted sesame seeds. Although light sesame oil is suitable for cooking, it lacks the characteristic flavor of the dark variety.

• Like olive oil, dark sesame oil is low in saturated fat and is thus considered a healthy fat choice. In addition, since a little of this intensely flavored oil goes a long way in flavoring a dish, you can get maximum taste from just a few calories-worth. Try drizzling a little over steamed vegetables, sprinkling a few drops into broth-based, ginger-spiked soups, or use it to perk up scrambled eggs and omelets.

• Look for dark sesame oil (also known as toasted sesame oil or Asian sesame oil) in the Asian or natural foods section of supermarkets. Once opened, the oil can be stored in the refrigerator up to 4 months.

# TORTELLINI STEW WITH SPINACH AND TOMATO

*For supper in a snap, try this throw-together pasta dish. Chicken broth is used to cook the tortellini and helps make a flavorful sauce when juicy canned tomatoes and spinach are added. A sprinkling of cheese provides a tasty finish.*

1 (14-oz.) can reduced-sodium vegetable or
   chicken broth
1 (9-oz.) pkg. refrigerated cheese or mushroom
   tortellini
1 (14.5-oz.) can diced tomatoes
3 cups packed baby spinach
3 tablespoons chopped fresh basil
2 tablespoons freshly shredded Asiago or
   Parmesan cheese
⅛ teaspoon freshly ground pepper

▶ Bring broth to a boil in medium saucepan over high heat. Add tortellini. Reduce heat to medium-low; simmer gently 5 minutes.

▶ Gently stir in tomatoes; simmer 4 minutes or until tortellini is tender. Stir in spinach 1 cup at a time just until wilted. Stir in basil.

▶ Ladle into shallow bowls; sprinkle with cheese and pepper.

**WINE** Serve a medium-bodied red with this stew.

**2 (2½-cup) servings**
PER SERVING: 295 calories, 11.5 g total fat (5.5 g saturated fat), 14.5 g protein, 34.5 g carbohydrate, 110 mg cholesterol, 710 mg sodium, 4 g fiber

# TRIPLE GINGER-PEAR BREAD PUDDING

*Three forms of ginger (grated fresh, ground and crystallized) give surprising pizzazz to the mellow custard and sweet fruit flavor of this pudding. You can vary the quantity of each type of ginger to suit your own taste, or kick it up a notch if you wish. Peaches, nectarines or apricots can be substituted for the pears.*

### BREAD MIXTURE

6 cups lightly packed cubed (1½ inch) challah or Italian
    country bread
2 cups milk
⅓ cup sugar
1½ teaspoons ground ginger
½ teaspoon nutmeg
1 teaspoon vanilla
½ cup golden raisins

### CUSTARD

4 eggs, room temperature
1 cup whipping cream
¼ cup sugar
¼ cup finely chopped crystallized ginger
2 teaspoons grated fresh ginger
½ teaspoon ground ginger
½ teaspoon plus ⅛ teaspoon nutmeg
½ teaspoon salt

### FRUIT

2 large Anjou, Bosc or Bartlett pears, peeled, cut into
    ¾-inch pieces (about 2 cups)
1 cup apricot preserves

▶ Heat broiler. Place bread in 15x10x1-inch pan. Broil 4 to 6 inches from heat 2 to 3 minutes or until golden, turning once. Watch carefully to prevent burning.

▶ Heat oven to 350°F. Grease 2-quart glass baking dish. In large bowl, whisk together all remaining bread mixture ingredients except raisins. Stir in toasted bread and raisins. Let stand 3 to 5 minutes, stirring occasionally, until liquid is absorbed. Add pears; stir gently to mix. Spread mixture evenly in baking dish. Spoon preserves over bread mixture.

▶ In same large bowl, whisk eggs until mixed. Add all remaining custard ingredients; whisk until blended. Pour over bread mixture, making sure custard evenly coats bread. Sprinkle additional ⅛ teaspoon nutmeg over top.

▶ Bake 65 to 70 minutes or until top is puffed and knife inserted in center comes out almost clean. Cool slightly on wire rack. Serve warm. Refrigerate leftovers.

**BEER** Grant's Scottish Ale from Washington is rich with lots of hops to give a slightly bitter edge to this dish.

**12 servings**
PER SERVING: 320 calories, 10 g total fat (5 g saturated fat), 6 g protein, 54.5 g carbohydrate, 105 mg cholesterol, 200 mg sodium, 2 g fiber

# Cozy Comfort Food

*Try these classic winter warm-ups built for two.*

## PORK CHOPS WITH CRANBERRY-SAGE CHUTNEY

*While high-quality canned cranberry sauce works well in the chutney, fresh cranberry sauce adds an extra spark of flavor. If you'd like, substitute boneless skinless chicken breast halves or sliced turkey breast for the pork chops.*

2 (6-oz.) boneless pork loin chops, 1 inch thick

¼ teaspoon salt

¼ teaspoon freshly ground pepper

1 tablespoon chopped fresh sage, divided

1½ tablespoons unsalted butter, divided

¼ cup minced shallots

½ cup white wine or cranberry juice

½ cup canned or fresh whole berry cranberry sauce

Sage leaves for garnish

▶ Sprinkle both sides of pork chops with salt and pepper; sprinkle with ½ tablespoon of the chopped sage, pressing lightly into meat.

▶ Melt 1 tablespoon of the butter in medium skillet over medium-high heat. Add pork; cook 6 to 8 minutes or until golden brown and center is light pink, turning once. Place on plate.

▶ Melt remaining ½ tablespoon butter in same skillet over medium heat. Add shallots; cook and stir 30 seconds. Add wine; bring to a boil, scraping up any browned bits from bottom of skillet. Boil 1 to 2 minutes or until reduced by half. Stir in cranberry sauce and remaining ½ tablespoon chopped sage; bring to a simmer. Return pork to skillet; simmer 1 to 2 minutes or until pork is no longer pink in center and chutney is lightly thickened.

▶ Place pork on plates. Spoon chutney over pork; garnish with sage leaves.

**WINE** Try a lighter, fruit-filled red.

**2 servings**
PER SERVING: 475 calories, 21.5 g total fat (10 g saturated fat), 37 g protein, 29.5 g carbohydrate, 130 mg cholesterol, 385 mg sodium, 1.5 g fiber

# CLAM AND POTATO CHOWDER

*Chowder comes from the French word chaudière, the pot in which hearty fishermen's soups are cooked. True chowders typically include potatoes, and many of them contain seafood. This recipe uses juice from the clams for part of the liquid. If you don't get ¹/₂ cup juice, increase the amount of bottled clam juice.*

2 slices bacon, cut into 1-inch pieces

1 small onion, chopped

1 rib celery, chopped

¹/₂ cup chopped fennel, fronds removed and
   reserved for garnish

8 oz. red potatoes, diced (¹/₂ inch)

12 oz. chopped fresh clams or canned clams,
   drained, juice reserved

²/₃ cup white wine

²/₃ cup whipping cream

²/₃ cup clam juice

1 tablespoon chopped fresh tarragon

¹/₄ teaspoon salt

¹/₄ teaspoon freshly ground pepper

▶ In medium saucepan, cook bacon over medium heat 3 minutes or until crisp, stirring frequently. Place on paper towels to drain.

▶ Add onion, celery and chopped fennel to saucepan containing bacon drippings. Cook over medium heat 4 minutes or just until softened, stirring frequently. Add potatoes; cook and stir 1 minute. Add juice from clams (about ¹/₂ cup) and half of the cooked bacon; reduce heat to medium-low. Cover and simmer 8 to 10 minutes or until potatoes are tender.

▶ Add wine. Increase heat to medium; bring to a boil. Add cream, ²/₃ cup clam juice, tarragon, salt and pepper; bring just to a simmer. Simmer 8 minutes. Add clams; heat 30 to 60 seconds or until clams are hot.

▶ Ladle soup into 2 large deep bowls. Sprinkle with remaining half of the bacon; garnish with fennel fronds.

**WINE** This rich, creamy chowder pairs well with Chardonnay.

**2 (2¹/₄-cup) servings**
PER SERVING: 675 calories, 45.5 g total fat (23 g saturated fat), 28.5 g protein, 36 g carbohydrate, 170 mg cholesterol, 735 mg sodium, 4 g fiber

# HERBED DROP BISCUITS

*These light, buttery biscuits are enlivened with a delicate hint of herbs. The recipe can be doubled if you're serving guests.*

**⅔ cup all-purpose flour**

**1 tablespoon chopped fresh herbs**

**1 teaspoon sugar**

**1 teaspoon baking powder**

**¼ teaspoon salt**

**⅛ teaspoon freshly ground pepper**

**2 tablespoons unsalted butter, chilled, cut up**

**⅓ cup whole milk**

▶ Heat oven to 450°F.

▶ Spray small baking sheet with nonstick cooking spray or line with parchment paper.

▶ In medium bowl, whisk together flour, herbs, sugar, baking powder, salt and pepper. With pastry blender or 2 knives, cut in butter until mixture resembles coarse crumbs with some pea-sized pieces. With fork, stir in milk until moist dough forms. Spoon about ¼ cup dough for each biscuit onto baking sheet, keeping biscuits at least 2 inches apart.

▶ Bake 10 to 13 minutes or until bottoms are golden brown. Serve warm.

**4 biscuits**
PER BISCUIT: 145 calories, 6.5 g total fat (4 g saturated fat), 3 g protein, 18.5 g carbohydrate, 20 mg cholesterol, 280 mg sodium, .5 g fiber

# SUNDAY SUPPER CHICKEN

*Browning the chicken and vegetables gives this stew an extra layer of flavor. While it's worthy of Sunday dinner, it's easy enough for a weeknight meal. Serve the dish over biscuits, mashed potatoes or rice.*

2 tablespoons all-purpose flour

¼ teaspoon salt

¼ teaspoon freshly ground pepper

8 oz. boneless skinless chicken breast halves
   or thighs, cut into 1- to 1½-inch pieces

2 tablespoons unsalted butter, divided

4 oz. baby carrots (about 1 cup)

1 cup sliced parsnips (½ inch)

1 leek, white and light green parts, sliced
   (about ½ cup)

1 (14-oz.) can reduced-sodium chicken broth

1 tablespoon chopped fresh thyme

▶ Place flour, salt and pepper in small resealable plastic bag; shake to mix. Add chicken pieces in batches; toss to lightly coat. Remove chicken from flour mixture; reserve any remaining flour mixture.

▶ Melt 1 tablespoon of the butter in large deep skillet over medium-high heat. Add chicken; cook 5 to 7 minutes or until golden brown on all sides, turning occasionally. Place on plate.

▶ Melt remaining 1 tablespoon butter in same skillet over medium heat. Add carrots, parsnips and leek; cook, stirring frequently, 7 to 10 minutes or until softened and edges are lightly browned. Stir in reserved flour mixture; cook and stir 1 minute. Stir in broth. Increase heat to high; bring to a boil. Boil 5 minutes or until broth is lightly thickened, stirring occasionally. Reduce heat to medium. Add chicken and thyme; simmer 2 to 3 minutes or until chicken is no longer pink in center. Serve in shallow bowls.

**WINE** A Chardonnay fits the bill here.

**2 servings**
PER SERVING: 390 calories, 16.5 g total fat (8.5 g saturated fat), 32 g protein, 28 g carbohydrate, 100 mg cholesterol, 795 mg sodium, 5.5 g fiber

133

# WARM CHOCOLATE TRUFFLE TART

*This tart may be modest in appearance, with a filling that's just ½ inch thick, but its taste is truly rich, chocolaty and just plain decadent. The pastry, made with melted butter, bakes up crisp, sweet and buttery. The combination is unbeatable.*

### CRUST

½ cup unsalted butter

¼ cup sugar

¾ teaspoon vanilla

⅛ teaspoon salt

1 cup all-purpose flour

### FILLING

5 tablespoons unsalted butter, cut up

½ cup sugar

¼ cup unsweetened cocoa

1 cup whipping cream

1¼ teaspoons instant espresso
    coffee powder

½ teaspoon vanilla

1 egg, lightly beaten

▶ Heat oven to 350°F. Melt ½ cup butter in medium saucepan over medium heat. Remove from heat; stir in ¼ cup sugar, ¾ teaspoon vanilla and ⅛ teaspoon salt. Add flour; mix just until well combined.

▶ Press dough in bottom and up sides of 9½-inch tart pan. Place pan on baking sheet. Bake 20 to 25 minutes or until deep golden brown.

▶ Meanwhile, melt 5 tablespoons butter in same medium saucepan over medium heat. Add ½ cup sugar, cocoa and cream. Cook over medium heat, stirring until mixture is smooth and small bubbles begin to form around edges. Remove from heat; stir in coffee powder and ½ teaspoon vanilla.

▶ Just before crust is done baking, whisk egg thoroughly into hot chocolate mixture. Remove crust from oven; pour filling into hot crust. Return to oven; bake an additional 10 to 12 minutes or until barely set. (Filling will quiver slightly when tapped at side.) Cool in pan on wire rack 25 minutes. Serve tart warm or at room temperature. Store in refrigerator.

**8 servings**
PER SERVING: 400 calories, 29 g total fat (18 g saturated fat), 4 g protein, 33.5 g carbohydrate, 110 mg cholesterol, 55 mg sodium, 1.5 g fiber

135

## LEMON-ROASTED CHICKEN THIGHS

*Chicken thighs are baked in a lemon-rich sauce for a simple weeknight meal. This method basically steams the chicken, producing moist and tender results. Serve the dish with mashed potatoes drizzled with extra sauce.*

**2 tablespoons olive oil, divided**

**4 boneless skinless chicken thighs**

**3 tablespoons fresh lemon juice**

**1 garlic clove, chopped**

**¼ teaspoon salt**

**⅛ teaspoon freshly ground pepper**

**⅛ teaspoon dried Italian seasoning or oregano**

**2 tablespoons chopped fresh parsley**

▶ Heat oven to 400°F. Heat large skillet over medium-high heat until hot. Add 1 tablespoon of the oil; heat until hot. Add chicken; cook 3 to 5 minutes or until browned, turning once. Place in shallow baking dish.

▶ In small bowl, whisk together lemon juice, remaining 1 tablespoon oil, garlic, salt, pepper and Italian seasoning. Pour evenly over chicken. Bake, uncovered, 15 to 20 minutes or until no longer pink in center, turning once.

▶ Sprinkle chicken with parsley; serve with pan juices.

**WINE**  Pair this dish with an earthy, dry white, such as Sauvignon Blanc.

**2 servings**
PER SERVING: 350 calories, 24.5 g total fat (5.5 g saturated fat), 29 g protein, 2.5 g carbohydrate, 85 mg cholesterol, 380 mg sodium, .5 g fiber

# PEPPER-SMOTHERED SKIRT STEAK

*Skirt steak, cut from the underside of the animal, is boneless and lean. It's similar in texture to flank steak but smaller, narrower and longer. Both cuts benefit greatly from overnight marinating and brief cooking (to no more than medium-rare).*

1 (1-lb.) beef skirt or flank steak, cut into
2 pieces

2 tablespoons lemon juice

1 teaspoon coriander seeds, crushed

½ teaspoon five-spice powder

¼ teaspoon freshly ground black pepper

¼ teaspoon white pepper

¼ teaspoon salt

1 tablespoon vegetable oil

1 small onion, thinly sliced

1 green bell pepper, thinly sliced

1 tablespoon soy sauce

▶ Sprinkle steaks with lemon juice. In small bowl, stir together coriander seeds, five-spice powder, black pepper, white pepper and salt. Sprinkle over both sides of steaks, pressing to adhere. Place steaks in resealable plastic bag; refrigerate 8 hours or overnight.

▶ Heat oil in large skillet over medium heat until hot. Add onion; cook 3 minutes. Add bell pepper; cook 7 minutes or until browned and tender, stirring occasionally. Remove from heat; sprinkle vegetables with soy sauce, stirring to combine.

▶ Heat broiler. Broil steaks 4 to 6 inches from heat 5 to 8 minutes for medium-rare or until of desired doneness, turning once. Place steaks on cutting board. Cover loosely with foil; let stand 5 minutes. Cut across the grain into thin slices. Serve topped with warm green pepper-onion mixture.

**BEER/WINE** A dark, spicy beer, such as Sierra Nevada Porter from California, works well. Or serve a spicy Zinfandel.

**2 servings**
PER SERVING: 455 calories, 23 g total fat (7 g saturated fat), 50.5 g protein, 10 g carbohydrate, 130 mg cholesterol, 870 mg sodium, 2.5 g fiber

# LEMON-CRUSTED HADDOCK WITH CORNICHON MAYONNAISE

*A mayonnaise peppered with tangy chopped cornichons (French pickled gherkins) turns a simple fish dish into a full-flavored meal. Delicate-textured white fish, such as haddock or cod, are best broiled or baked so that they don't have to be turned, which could cause them to break. Halibut is another good option.*

2 (8-oz.) haddock or cod fillets

3 teaspoons lemon juice, divided

1 tablespoon olive oil

¼ teaspoon salt

⅛ teaspoon freshly ground pepper

⅓ cup unseasoned dry bread crumbs

3 tablespoons mayonnaise

4 cornichons, coarsely chopped*

(1½ tablespoons)

¼ teaspoon paprika

▶ Heat oven to 425°F. Line baking sheet with foil; place fish fillets, skin side down, on baking sheet.

▶ In small bowl, stir together 2½ teaspoons of the lemon juice, oil, salt and pepper. Spoon mixture over fish. Sprinkle evenly with bread crumbs, patting slightly to help crumbs adhere. Bake 7 minutes or until fish just begins to flake.

▶ Meanwhile, in another small bowl, stir together mayonnaise, cornichons, paprika and remaining ½ teaspoon lemon juice. Serve fish with cornichon mayonnaise.

**TIP** If you can't find cornichons, use any small, tart pickle available.

**WINE** This full-flavored dish calls for a Chardonnay.

**2 servings**
PER SERVING: 420 calories, 26 g total fat (4 g saturated fat), 31 g protein, 14.5 g carbohydrate, 90 mg cholesterol, 775 mg sodium, .5 g fiber

# MUSHROOM-TOMATO PASTA WITH ARUGULA

*Crimini mushrooms imbue this pasta with earthy notes that are a good match for the creamy melted cheese. Criminis, frequently labeled as baby portobellos, have a darker color and deeper flavor than the white button variety.*

2 tablespoons butter

8 oz. crimini mushrooms, sliced (¼ inch)

1 large garlic clove, chopped

¼ teaspoon salt

⅛ teaspoon freshly ground pepper

1 cup grape tomatoes or small cherry tomatoes, halved

1½ teaspoons chopped fresh sage

½ cup reduced-sodium vegetable broth

4 oz. penne or other tube-shaped pasta

2 cups packed coarsely chopped arugula or spinach

½ cup (2 oz.) shredded fontina cheese

2 tablespoons freshly grated Parmesan cheese

▶ Melt butter in large skillet over medium high heat. Add mushrooms, garlic, salt and pepper; cook 3 to 4 minutes or until mushrooms soften, stirring frequently. Add tomatoes and sage. Reduce heat to low; cook 3 to 5 minutes or until tomatoes soften, stirring occasionally. Add broth. Increase heat to medium-high; cook 4 to 5 minutes or until slightly thickened and reduced by half. Remove from heat; cover skillet to keep sauce warm.

▶ Meanwhile, cook penne in large pot of boiling salted water according to package directions; drain, reserving 2 tablespoons pasta cooking water.

▶ Place arugula in large bowl. Add pasta and reserved cooking water; toss. Stir in mushroom-tomato sauce. Add fontina cheese and Parmesan cheese; toss well.

**2 (2½-cup) servings**
PER SERVING: 515 calories, 24 g total fat (12.5 g saturated fat), 22 g protein, 56 g carbohydrate, 70 mg cholesterol, 1015 mg sodium, 6 g fiber

# CHOCOLATE OMNIPOTENCE

*Indulge yourself in this sophisticated, chocolaty dessert.*

**12 oz. semisweet chocolate, chopped**

**3 oz. bittersweet chocolate, chopped**

**2 cups sour cream, room temperature**

**¼ cup cognac or orange juice**

**1 cup heavy whipping cream**

**·1 teaspoon vanilla**

**8 purchased thin rolled cookies**

▶ Place 11 oz. of the semisweet chocolate and bittersweet chocolate in heatproof medium bowl. Bring 1 inch water to a boil in medium saucepan. Remove from heat. Place bowl of chocolate over water (bowl should not touch water). Let stand until chocolate is melted.

▶ Place sour cream in large bowl. Whisk in melted chocolate and cognac.

▶ Cut remaining 1 oz. semisweet chocolate into thin shavings with knife; stir half into chocolate mixture. Spoon into small bowls or stemmed glasses. Refrigerate at least 3 hours.

▶ In medium bowl, beat cream and vanilla at medium-high speed until stiff peaks form. Top each serving with whipped cream. Garnish with remaining shaved chocolate and cookies. Refrigerate leftovers.

**8 servings**
PER SERVING: 515 calories, 38.5 g total fat (22.5 g saturated fat), 5 g protein, 42.5 g carbohydrate, 75 mg cholesterol, 80 mg sodium, 3.5 g fiber

143

# No-Stress Dinners

*These easy-to-make dishes are the perfect ending to a busy day.*

# HEARTY PASTA WITH TOMATOES AND GARBANZO BEANS

*Keep canned tomatoes and beans in your pantry for a satisfying pasta supper that can be made in less than 30 minutes. The onion is quickly sliced into attractive vertical strips to save time.*

**4 oz. (1 cup) rotini (spiral pasta)**

**1 tablespoon olive oil**

**1 small onion, sliced lengthwise**

**1 (14.5-oz.) can diced tomatoes**

**1 (7½-oz.) can garbanzo beans, drained, rinsed**

**½ teaspoon sugar**

**¼ teaspoon Italian seasoning**

**¼ teaspoon kosher (coarse) salt**

**⅛ teaspoon freshly ground pepper**

**¼ cup (1 oz.) freshly grated Parmesan cheese**

▶ Cook rotini in large pot of boiling salted water according to package directions; drain.

▶ Meanwhile, heat oil in large nonstick skillet over medium-high heat until hot. Add onion; cook 3 minutes or until lightly browned. Add all remaining ingredients except cheese. Reduce heat to low; cover and simmer 5 minutes or until flavors have blended. Toss rotini with sauce; sprinkle with cheese.

**WINE** Serve a lighter, slightly spicy Chianti with this dish.

**2 (2-cup) servings**
PER SERVING: 510 calories, 13.5 g total fat (3.5 g saturated fat), 21 g protein, 77 g carbohydrate, 10 mg cholesterol, 1015 mg sodium, 10.5 g fiber

*144*

# ORANGE-GLAZED CHICKEN

*A quick orange pan sauce beautifully glazes and flavors chicken breasts. To save time, grate oranges when you have extra ones and freeze the peel in a small jar. Microwave it briefly to thaw it.*

½ cup reduced-sodium chicken broth

2 tablespoons orange marmalade

2 teaspoons lemon juice

1 teaspoon grated orange peel

¾ teaspoon cornstarch

¼ teaspoon dried basil

¼ teaspoon kosher (coarse) salt

⅛ teaspoon freshly ground pepper

1 tablespoon olive oil

2 boneless skinless chicken breast halves

▶ In medium bowl, whisk together broth, marmalade, lemon juice, orange peel, cornstarch, basil, salt and pepper.

▶ Heat oil in large nonstick skillet over medium-high heat until hot. Add chicken; cook 5 minutes or until golden brown, turning once. Add broth mixture. Reduce heat to medium-low; cover and simmer 8 minutes or until chicken is no longer pink in center.

**WINE**  Pair this chicken with a lighter Chardonnay that doesn't have too much oak.

**2 servings**
PER SERVING: 275 calories, 10.5 g total fat (2 g saturated fat), 27.5 g protein, 15.5 g carbohydrate, 75 mg cholesterol, 410 mg sodium, .5 g fiber

---

## COOKING CHICKEN

Try these tips for preparing perfect chicken breasts:

• Season chicken with salt just before cooking. Salt immediately begins drawing out the juices; if the meat is allowed to stand too long, it will result in chicken that is dry, less tender and difficult to brown.

• When sautéing chicken, heat the pan until it is hot; then add the oil and heat it briefly before adding the chicken. This helps keep the meat from sticking to the pan.

• Brown the chicken on medium-high heat on one side before turning. If the chicken sticks, continue cooking for an extra minute or two before turning it. Sticking usually means it needs a little extra cooking time. For thick pieces, reduce the heat to medium to continue through cooking.

• To check for doneness, press on the chicken breast with a fork. The meat should feel slightly firm but still have a bit of spring to it. When its pierced, the juices should run clear and the meat should no longer be pink.

# STRIP STEAKS WITH SHALLOTS

*A simple sauce enhances the meaty flavor of good steaks. Pan juices and beef broth give it richness, while minced shallots provide a subtle onion flavor.*

½ cup reduced-sodium beef broth
¾ teaspoon Dijon mustard
¾ teaspoon Worcestershire sauce
½ teaspoon all-purpose flour
¼ teaspoon kosher (coarse) salt
⅛ teaspoon freshly ground pepper
1 tablespoon olive oil
2 (6-oz.) New York strip steaks
   (¾ inch thick)
2 tablespoons minced shallots

▶ In small bowl, whisk together broth, mustard, Worcestershire sauce, flour, salt and pepper.

▶ Heat oil in heavy large skillet over medium-high heat until hot. Add steaks; cook 6 to 8 minutes for medium-rare or until of desired doneness, turning once. Place on platter.

▶ Reduce heat to medium-low. Add shallots; cook and stir 1 minute or until lightly browned. Add broth mixture; increase heat to medium. Bring to a boil; boil 1 minute or until slightly thickened. Serve sauce over steaks.

**WINE** Cabernet Sauvignon and steak are perfect partners.

**2 servings**
PER SERVING: 350 calories, 18.5 g total fat (5.5 g saturated fat), 40.5 g protein, 2.5 g carbohydrate, 75 mg cholesterol, 365 mg sodium, .5 g fiber

---

## COOKING STEAK

Follow these steps when broiling, pan-frying or charcoal-grilling steak:

• For better browning, pat the steak dry with a paper towel before cooking.

• Don't salt steaks before browning. The salt draws out the moisture, inhibiting browning, and makes the steak less juicy.

• Wait until after a steak is cooked to trim off the fat. Cooking with the fat adds flavor and helps it retain the juices.

• When pan-frying more than one steak, make sure the skillet is large enough. If the steaks are too crowded, they will steam instead of brown.

• Use tongs to handle the steak. Don't pierce it with a fork, which allows juices to escape and could result in drier meat.

• Transfer the cooked steak to a platter or cutting board, and wait at least 5 minutes before slicing it. During the delay, the meat will relax and the juices will redistribute in the meat.

# PORK MEDALLIONS WITH MUSHROOMS AND ROSEMARY

*Pieces of pork tenderloin are flattened into medallions, lightly breaded and topped with a tasty mushroom-tomato sauce. Tubes of tomato paste, shelved near the other tomato products in stores, are convenient for recipes like this that call for a small amount. Just squeeze out what you need and store the tube in the refrigerator.*

⅔ cup reduced-sodium chicken broth

1 tablespoon tomato paste

¼ teaspoon dried rosemary, crushed

¼ teaspoon kosher (coarse) salt

⅛ teaspoon freshly ground pepper

8 oz. pork tenderloin, cut croswise into
   4 pieces

1 tablespoon seasoned dry bread crumbs

1 tablespoon olive oil

1½ cups sliced mushrooms

▶ In medium bowl, gradually whisk broth into tomato paste. Stir in rosemary, salt and pepper. Flatten pork to 1-inch thickness; lightly coat pork with bread crumbs.

▶ Heat oil in large nonstick skillet over medium-high heat until hot. Add pork; cook 6 minutes or until golden brown, turning once. Place on plate.

▶ Reduce heat to medium. Add mushrooms to same skillet; cook 3 minutes or until lightly browned. Return pork to skillet; add broth mixture. Reduce heat to low; cover and simmer 2 to 4 minutes or until pork is pale pink in center. Place pork on plate.

▶ Increase heat to high; boil sauce 2 to 3 minutes or until reduced and slightly thickened. Serve sauce over pork.

**WINE**  Look for medium-bodied Merlot with moderate tannins.

**2 servings**
PER SERVING: 245 calories, 11.5 g total fat (2.5 g saturated fat), 29 g protein, 6 g carbohydrate, 70 mg cholesterol, 525 mg sodium, 1.5 g fiber

# MAUNA KEA CHOCOLATE CAKE

*Coffee, chocolate and vanilla, all grown in Hawaii, are featured prominently in this cake, cut to resemble the mountains that dominate the landscape. The dessert can be baked a day or two ahead, then cut, glazed and refrigerated until ready to serve.*

### CAKE

½ cup strong coffee

3 oz. semisweet chocolate, chopped

¾ cup milk

½ teaspoon lemon juice or vinegar

½ cup unsalted butter, softened

1½ cups sugar

2 eggs

1 teaspoon baking soda

1 teaspoon vanilla

1½ cups all-purpose flour

### SAUCE

2 egg yolks

3 tablespoons sugar

1 cup milk

½ teaspoon vanilla

### GLAZE

6 oz. semisweet chocolate, chopped

3 tablespoons unsalted butter

3 tablespoons strong coffee

1 teaspoon corn syrup

1 teaspoon vanilla

▶ Heat oven to 375°F. Spray 13x9-inch pan with nonstick cooking spray. Line bottom with parchment paper; spray and flour paper and pan. In small saucepan over medium heat, bring ½ cup coffee to just below a simmer. Remove from heat; add 3 oz. chocolate. Let stand until chocolate is melted; stir. Let stand until cool. In small bowl, combine milk and lemon juice; set aside.

▶ In large bowl, beat ½ cup butter and 1½ cups sugar at medium speed until light and fluffy. Add eggs one at a time, beating until mixture is creamy. Beat in chocolate mixture and milk mixture. Stir in baking soda and 1 teaspoon vanilla.

▶ Sift flour over batter; fold just until flour is blended. Pour into pan.

▶ Bake 30 minutes or until toothpick inserted in center comes out clean. Cool in pan on wire rack 20 minutes. Run small knife around outside edge to loosen; invert cake onto wire rack. Cool completely. Remove parchment paper.

▶ Meanwhile, in small saucepan, combine egg yolks and 3 tablespoons sugar. Stir in 1 cup milk. Cook over low heat just until mixture comes to a boil and coats back of spoon, stirring constantly. Immediately remove from heat. Stir in ½ teaspoon vanilla. Pour into medium bowl. Place plastic wrap directly on surface; refrigerate to cool.

▶ Meanwhile, in medium saucepan, combine 6 oz. chocolate, 3 tablespoons butter, 3 tablespoons coffee and corn syrup. Heat over low heat until melted and smooth, stirring frequently. Stir in 1 teaspoon vanilla.

▶ Place wire rack over baking sheet. Cut cooled cake in half lengthwise. Cut each strip crosswise into thirds. Cut each square diagonally (you will end up with 12 triangles). Remove any loose crumbs; set each triangle, long side down, on wire rack. Spoon about 2 teaspoons glaze over each triangle, spreading glaze with small spatula. (Reserve remaining glaze to decorate plates.)

▶ To serve, heat remaining glaze until warm. Place about 2 tablespoons vanilla sauce on each dessert plate, swirling gently to distribute sauce. Place cake in center of sauce on each plate. Spoon 3 large drops of glaze around front of each plate. Run toothpick or end of chopstick through each drop to form a sideways S, like a wave. For a tropical touch, garnish with an edible orchid or other edible blossom.

**WINE**  With its sweet caramel-like fruit flavors, Port is a successful match with this cake.

**12 servings**
PER SERVING: 405 calories, 19.5 g total fat (11.5 g saturated fat), 5.5 g protein, 56 g carbohydrate, 100 mg cholesterol, 140 mg sodium, 1.5 g fiber

# Small is Beautiful

*The only thing pared down about these entrees is the size.*
*They're definitely full flavor!*

## PERSONAL MEAT LOAVES

*The real advantage in having your own "personal" meat loaf is not having to share the coveted, crusty end pieces with anyone! Serve with mashed or baked potatoes and steamed green beans, or pick up on the loaves' Southwestern flavor by stirring green onions, corn and sour cream into the potatoes and sprinkling the beans with finely diced pimiento or roasted red bell pepper. Most supermarkets carry a meat loaf mix of lean ground beef, pork and veal. You can substitute ground turkey with good results, too.*

1 tablespoon olive oil

½ cup chopped onion

1 tablespoon chili powder

½ teaspoon ground cumin

10 oz. lean ground meat loaf mix (equal parts
    ground beef, pork and veal)

¼ cup unseasoned dry bread crumbs

¼ cup chopped fresh cilantro

½ teaspoon salt

¼ teaspoon freshly ground pepper

1 egg

2 tablespoons hickory-smoked barbecue sauce

▶ Heat oven to 350°F. Heat oil in small skillet over medium heat until hot. Add onion; cook 5 minutes or until softened, stirring frequently. Add chili powder and cumin; cook 1 minute. Remove from heat; cool 5 minutes.

▶ In medium bowl, combine ground meat, bread crumbs, cilantro, salt, pepper, egg and cooked onion mixture. With hands, mix gently but thoroughly.

▶ Divide mixture in half. Shape each half into free-form loaf about 4 inches long. Place in shallow glass baking dish or pie plate. Spread tops with barbecue sauce. (Recipe can be prepared up to 4 hours ahead. Cover and refrigerate. An additional 5 to 10 minutes baking time may be needed if meat loaf mixture has been refrigerated.)

▶ Bake 35 to 45 minutes or until no longer pink in center.

**WINE/BEER**  The slightly smoky-sweet barbecue sauce on the meat loaves cries out for a juicy, gutsy red, such as a good Grenache-Shiraz. The dish also goes well with the creamy, hoppy flavors of the dark Anchor Porter.

**2 servings**
PER SERVING: 440 calories, 26.5 g total fat (8 g saturated fat), 31.5 g protein, 18 g carbohydrate, 195 mg cholesterol, 965 mg sodium, 3 g fiber

# SHRIMP AND FENNEL OVER LINGUINE

*Scallops also pair well with fennel and can replace shrimp in this dish, as could calamari or even lobster meat if you have a cause for celebration. Shellfish cook very quickly, so whatever option you use, add it at the very end. Complete this simple supper with an arugula salad tossed with a creamy Gorgonzola dressing, and serve a basket of crusty Italian bread.*

1 tablespoon olive oil

1 cup thinly sliced fennel bulb, fronds removed

1 cup coarsely chopped onion

3 large garlic cloves, minced

¼ teaspoon salt

¼ to ½ teaspoon crushed red pepper

1 (14½-oz.) can Italian-style diced tomatoes, undrained

⅓ to ½ cup white wine or bottled clam juice

½ lb. shelled, deveined uncooked medium shrimp

¼ cup chopped fresh basil

¼ cup chopped fresh Italian parsley

4½ oz. fresh linguine (from 9-oz. pkg.)

▶ Heat oil in large skillet over medium heat until hot. Add fennel and onion; cook 5 to 6 minutes or until softened, stirring frequently.

▶ Stir in garlic, salt and crushed red pepper. Cook 1 minute. Add tomatoes and 1/3 cup wine. Simmer, uncovered, 5 minutes or until slightly thickened. If mixture seems too thick, add remaining wine. Gently stir in shrimp, basil and parsley. Cook 3 minutes or until shrimp turn pink.

▶ Meanwhile, cook linguine according to package directions; drain well. Toss linguine with hot shrimp mixture.

**WINE**  A crisp white with a flinty, smoky edge will reinforce this dish's flavors. For a red alternative, a ripe Chianti plays off the tomato notes.

**2 servings**
PER SERVING: 520 calories, 9.5 g total fat (1.5 g saturated fat), 30 g protein, 78.5 g carbohydrate, 160 mg cholesterol, 1350 mg sodium, 7 g fiber

# ROASTED BANANA BREAD PUDDING WITH BOURBON-PRALINE SAUCE

*Baked in individual ramekins, this flavorful warm dessert can be served in its dish or unmolded onto a dessert plate. The contrast between the mildly sweet banana flavor and the intense praline sauce is dazzling and transforms the humble pudding into a party show-stopper. Serve with softly whipped cream, if desired.*

### BREAD MIXTURE

4 cups lightly packed cubed (¾ inch) challah or
   French bread

5 firm ripe bananas

1½ cups milk

⅓ cup packed light brown sugar

1 teaspoon cinnamon

½ teaspoon nutmeg

### CUSTARD

3 eggs, room temperature

1 cup whipping cream

⅓ cup packed light brown sugar

1 tablespoon bourbon or dark rum,
   if desired

1 teaspoon vanilla

¼ teaspoon salt

2 teaspoons sugar

### SAUCE

½ cup coarsely chopped pecans

2 tablespoons unsalted butter

½ cup packed dark brown sugar

½ cup whipping cream

2 tablespoons milk

2 tablespoons cornstarch

1 tablespoon bourbon or dark rum,
   if desired

1 teaspoon vanilla

Dash salt

▶ Heat broiler. Generously butter 8 (½-cup) ovenproof ramekins or custard cups. Place ramekins in large shallow pan; ramekins should not touch each other.

▶ Place bread in 15x10x1-inch pan. Broil 4 to 6 inches from heat 2 to 3 minutes or until golden brown, turning once. Watch carefully to prevent burning.

▶ Heat oven to 425°F. Lightly butter 8-inch square baking pan. Set 1 banana aside for garnish. Peel remaining 4 bananas; place in pan. Bake at 425°F. for 10 to 12 minutes or until soft and slightly browned.

▶ Reduce oven temperature to 350°F. Place 2 baked bananas in medium bowl; mash with fork. Let remaining 2 baked bananas cool slightly; cut into ¼-inch slices. (Bananas are very soft but can be sliced.) Place 3 or 4 slices in bottom of each ramekin.

▶ In large bowl, whisk together all remaining bread mixture ingredients except reserved banana. Whisk in mashed bananas. Stir in toasted bread. Let stand 4 to 5 minutes or until liquid is absorbed, stirring occasionally.

▶ In separate large bowl, whisk eggs until mixed. Add all remaining custard ingredients except 2 teaspoons sugar; whisk until blended. Spoon scant ⅓ cup soaked bread mixture into each ramekin, filling nearly to top; do not pack. Pour custard over bread mixture in each ramekin. Sprinkle with 2 teaspoons sugar.

▶ Place ramekins in large shallow pan; fill pan with hot water to about ⅓ way up sides of ramekins. Bake at 350°F. for 45 minutes or until tops are puffed and knife inserted in center comes out clean. Remove puddings from water bath; place on wire rack to cool slightly.

▶ Meanwhile, to prepare sauce, place pecans and butter in heavy medium saucepan. Cook over medium heat 4 minutes or until nuts are toasted, stirring frequently. Add ½ cup dark brown sugar and ½ cup cream; stir until smooth. In small bowl, blend 2 tablespoons milk and cornstarch. Stir cornstarch mixture into sauce. Increase heat to medium-high; cook until mixture comes to a boil, stirring constantly. Boil 2 minutes or until thickened, stirring constantly. Remove from heat; stir in 1 tablespoon bourbon, 1 teaspoon vanilla and dash salt. Serve warm. (Store sauce, covered, in refrigerator. If too thick after reheating, stir in 1 to 2 tablespoons milk.)

▶ Diagonally slice reserved banana. Serve puddings warm in ramekins, topped by warm sauce and garnished with banana. Or to unmold, run knife around sides of each ramekin; top each with dessert plate and invert with sharp downward motion. Turn puddings right side up onto plate. Refrigerate leftovers.

**BEER** Try Sierra Nevada Porter from California, a rich, chocolaty beer that has roasted qualities.

**8 servings**
PER SERVING: 520 calories, 26 g total fat (12.5 g saturated fat), 8 g protein, 66.5 g carbohydrate, 150 mg cholesterol, 220 mg sodium, 3 g fiber

# INDEX

## A

**Apples**
Baked Mustard-Apple Chicken Breasts, 112
Caramel Apple Bread Pudding, 86
Apricot & Balsamic Glazed Salmon, 116
**Artichoke**
Shrimp and Artichoke Frittata, 68
Asparagus-Goat Cheese Omelet, 35

## B

Bacon and Cornbread Dressing, 108
Baked Mustard-Apple Chicken Breasts, 112
Balsamic Pork Chops and Peppers, 10
**Beans**
canned
Hearty Pasta with Tomatoes and Garbanzo Beans, 144
Pasta with Tomatoes and Cannellini Beans, 101
Tuna, White Bean and Tomato Salad, 84
green
Mango-Glazed Green Beans, 18
**Beef**
Chimichurri Beef Steak, 42
Easy Beef Stroganoff, 19
Grilled Mini Meat Loaves, 40
Grilled Porterhouse Steak with Herb Butter, 24
Grilled Sirloin Steak with Sweet Onion and Bell Pepper Topping, 48
Pan-Seared Steaks with Mushroom-Cognac Sauce, 11
Pepper-Smothered Skirt Steak, 138
Personal Meat Loaf, 152–153
Sesame-Garlic Sirloin Steak, 120
Spice-Grilled Sirloin Steaks, 36
Strip Steaks with Shallots, 147
Thai Beef Salad, 72
**Berries**
Bumbleberry Pie, 30
Chocolate-Covered Berries, 67
Frozen Lemon-Lime Mousse with Berries, 46
Shortcut Strawberry Shortcake, 10
Spinach Salad with Grilled Pork Tenderloin and Strawberry Vinaigrette, 58
Strawberry-Orange Sundaes, 35
Violet Berry Fool, 78
**Biscuits**
Herbed Drop Biscuits, 131
Blackberry-Glazed Chicken Breasts, 18
Blueberries. See Berries
Blueberry Cornmeal Gems with Ginger Whipped Cream, 62
**Broccoli**
Penne with Sausage and Broccoli Raab, 92
Bumbleberry Pie, 30

**Butter**
Grilled Porterhouse Steak with Herb Butter, 24
Herbed Butter, 26
Buttermilk Pan-Fried Chicken, 93

## C

**Cakes**
Coffee Ice Cream Cookie Cake, 35
Lime Cheesecake with Fresh Fruit, 70
Mauna Kea Chocolate Cake, 150–151
Old-Fashioned New York Cheesecake with Strawberry Glaze, 14–15
Orange Gingerbread with Citrus Cream, 96
Shortcut Strawberry Shortcake, 10
Caramel Apple Bread Pudding, 86
Cheddar-Portobello Mushroom Skillet, 114
**Cheese**
Asparagus-Goat Cheese Omelet, 35
Cheddar-Portobello Mushroom Skillet, 114
Chunky Blue Cheese Vinaigrette, 51
Gorgonzola Toasts on the Grill, 43
Pilaf-Stuffed Eggplant with Mozzarella and Tomatoes, 52
Twice-Baked Cheddar Melts, 83
Chesapeake Bay Crab Cakes with Herbed Tartar Sauce, 28
**Chicken**
Baked Mustard-Apple Chicken Breasts, 112
Blackberry-Glazed Chicken Breasts, 18
Buttermilk Pan-Fried Chicken, 93
Chicken in Mojo Pan Sauce, 8
Chicken Saltimbocca, 74
Chicken with Olives, Tomatoes and Parsley, 34
Chicken with Orange, Rosemary and Nectarines, 50
Chicken with Spicy Fresh Tomato Sauce, 83
Citrus Grilled Chicken, 44
Coconut-Curry Chicken and Potatoes, 98
Grilled Honey Mustard Chicken Salad, 26
Lemon-Roasted Chicken Thighs, 136
Orange-Glazed Chicken, 146
Sunday Supper Chicken, 132
Warm Chicken Salad with Fresh Peaches, 64
Chicken in Mojo Pan Sauce, 8
Chicken Saltimbocca, 74
Chicken with Olives, Tomatoes and Parsley, 34
Chicken with Orange, Rosemary and Nectarines, 50
Chicken with Spicy Fresh Tomato Sauce, 83
Chimichurri Beef Steak, 42
**Chocolate**

Chocolate-Covered Berries, 67
Chocolate-Espresso Fudge Pie, 118
Chocolate Omnipotence, 142
Frozen Chocolate Cream Sabayon, 22
Mauna Kea Chocolate Cake, 150–151
Warm Chocolate Truffle Tart, 134
Chocolate-Covered Berries, 67
Chocolate-Espresso Fudge Pie, 118
Chocolate Omnipotence, 142
Chunky Blue Cheese Vinaigrette, 51
**Chutney**
Pork Chops with Cranberry-Sage Chutney, 128
Smoked Pork Chops with Spiced Raisin Chutney, 94
Citrus Grilled Chicken, 44
Clam and Potato Chowder, 130
Classic Crème Brulée, 104
Coconut-Curry Chicken and Potatoes, 98
Coffee Ice Cream Cookie Cake, 35
Cornmeal-Crusted Scallops with Corn Relish, 76
**Cozy Comfort Food**, 128–135
Clam and Potato Chowder, 130
Herbed Drop Biscuits, 131
Pork Chops with Cranberry-Sage Chutney, 128
Sunday Supper Chicken, 132
Warm Chocolate Truffle Tart, 134
**Cranberry**
Ginger Cranberry-Kumquat Relish, 109
Pork Chops with Cranberry-Sage Chutney, 128

## D

**Desserts**
Blueberry Cornmeal Gems with Ginger Whipped Cream, 62
Bumbleberry Pie, 30
Caramel Apple Bread Pudding, 86
Chocolate-Covered Berries, 67
Chocolate-Espresso Fudge Pie, 118
Chocolate Omnipotence, 142
Classic Crème Brulée, 104
Coffee Ice Cream Cookie Cake, 35
Frozen Chocolate Cream Sabayon, 22
Frozen Lemon-Lime Mousse with Berries, 46
Grilled Caramel Pineapple, 67
Lemon Meringue Pie, 38–39
Lime Cheesecake with Fresh Fruit, 70
Mauna Kea Chocolate Cake, 150–151
Old-Fashioned New York Cheesecake with Strawberry Glaze, 14–15
Orange Gingerbread with Citrus Cream, 96
Pecan Tarts, 111
Pistachio Ice Cream, 54

Roasted Banana Bread Pudding with Bourbon-Praline Sauce, 156–157
Shortcut Strawberry Shortcake, 10
Strawberry-Orange Sundaes, 35
Triple Ginger-Pear Bread Pudding, 126
Vanilla Ice Cream with Broiled Pineapple, 35
Violet Berry Fool, 78
Warm Chocolate Truffle Tart, 134
Warm Rhubarb Sundaes, 10
**Dining à Deux**, 16–23
Blackberry-Glazed Chicken Breasts, 18
Easy Beef Stroganoff, 19
Frozen Chocolate Cream Sabayon, 22
Pork Chops with Tarragon-Mustard Sauce, 16
Snapper in Parchment, 20
**Dinner in a Flash**, 8–15
Balsamic Pork Chops and Peppers, 10
Chicken in Mojo Pan Sauce, 8
Old-Fashioned New York Cheesecake with Strawberry Glaze, 14–15
Pan-Seared Steaks with Mushroom-Cognac Sauce, 11
Thai Shrimp Stir-Fry, 12
**Dressing**
Bacon and Cornbread Dressing, 108

## E

Easy Beef Stroganoff, 19
**Egg dishes**
Asparagus-Goat Cheese Omelet, 35
Huevos Rancheros Tostadas, 90
Roasted Banana Bread Pudding with Bourbon-Praline Sauce, 156–157
Shrimp and Artichoke Frittata, 68
Triple Ginger-Pear Bread Pudding, 126
**Eggplant**
Pilaf-Stuffed Eggplant with Mozzarella and Tomatoes, 52

## F

**Fish and Seafood**
Apricot & Balsamic Glazed Salmon, 116
Chesapeake Bay Crab Cakes with Herbed Tartar Sauce, 28
Clam and Potato Chowder, 130
Cornmeal-Crusted Scallops with Corn Relish, 76
Grilled Shrimp Wraps, 75
Halibut Steak with Lemon Glaze, 32
Lemon-Crusted Haddock with Cornichon Mayonnaise, 139
Miso-Glazed Salmon, 102
Sautéed Shrimp and Pasta with Sugar Snap Peas, 59
Shrimp and Artichoke Frittata, 68

Shrimp and Fennel over
Linguine, 154
Snapper in Parchment, 20
Thai Shrimp Stir-Fry, 12
Tuna, White Bean and Tomato
Salad, 84
**Fresh and Fast**, 80–87
Caramel Apple Bread Pudding,
86
Chicken with Spicy Fresh
Tomato Sauce, 83
Pork Chops with Peaches and
Basil, 80
Sausage and Peppers in Spanish
Rice, 82
Tuna, White Bean and Tomato
Salad, 84
Fresh Herb Vinaigrette, 51
**From Steak to Stew**, 120–127
Pan-Seared Lamb Chops with
Balsamic Glaze, 122
Red Curry Pork Tenderloin, 123
Sesame-Garlic Sirloin Steak, 120
Tortellini Stew with Spinach and
Tomato, 124
Triple Ginger-Pear Bread
Pudding, 126
Frozen Chocolate Cream Sabayon,
22
Frozen Lemon-Lime Mousse with
Berries, 46

**G**
Ginger Cranberry-Kumquat
Relish, 109
**Good for You, Too**, 98–105
Classic Créme Brulée, 104
Coconut-Curry Chicken and
Potatoes, 98
Lamb Patties with Yogurt
Sauce, 100
Miso-Glazed Salmon, 102
Pasta with Tomatoes and
Cannellini Beans, 101
Gorgonzola Toasts on the Grill, 43
Grilled Caramel Pineapple, 67
Grilled Honey Mustard Chicken
Salad, 26
Grilled Mini Meat Loaves, 40
Grilled Pizza Margherita, 43
Grilled Pork Chops with Cuban
Mojo Sauce, 56
Grilled Porterhouse Steak with
Herb Butter, 24
Grilled Potatoes with Malt
Vinegar, 43
Grilled Shrimp Wraps, 75
Grilled Sirloin Steak with Sweet
Onion and Bell Pepper Topping,
48
Grilled Summer Vegetables, 43
**Grilling**
Chimichurri Beef Steak, 42
Citrus Grilled Chicken, 44
Gorgonzola Toasts on the Grill,
43
Grilled Caramel Pineapple, 67
Grilled Honey Mustard Chicken
Salad, 26
Grilled Mini Meat Loaves, 40
Grilled Pork Chops with Cuban
Mojo Sauce, 56
Grilled Potatoes with Malt
Vinegar, 43
Grilled Shrimp Wraps, 75
Grilled Sirloin Steak with Sweet
Onion and Bell Pepper
Topping, 48

Grilled Summer Vegetables, 43
Spice-Grilled Sirloin Steaks, 36
Spinach Salad with Grilled Pork
Tenderloin and Strawberry
Vinaigrette, 58
Thai Beef Salad, 72
Warm Chicken Salad with Fresh
Peaches, 64

**H**
Halibut Steak with Lemon Glaze,
32
**Harvest Dinners**, 112–119
Apricot & Balsamic Glazed
Salmon, 116
Baked Mustard-Apple Chicken
Breasts, 112
Cheddar-Portobello Mushroom
Skillet, 114
Chocolate-Espresso Fudge Pie,
118
Moroccan Lamb Chops, 115
Hearty Pasta with Tomatoes and
Garbanzo Beans, 144
Herb-Brined Turkey Breast with
Bourbon Pan Gravy, 106–107
Herbed Butter, 26
Herbed Crumbs, 26
Herbed Drop Biscuits, 131
Herbed Olive Oil Vinaigrette, 26
Huevos Rancheros Tostadas, 90

**I**
**Ice cream dishes**
Coffee Ice Cream Cookie Cake,
35
Frozen Chocolate Cream
Sabayon, 22
Pistachio Ice Cream, 54
Strawberry-Orange Sundaes, 35
Vanilla Ice Cream with Broiled
Pineapple, 35
Warm Rhubarb Sundaes, 10
**An Intimate Holiday**, 106–111
Bacon and Cornbread Dressing,
108
Ginger Cranberry-Kumquat
Relish, 109
Herb-Brined Turkey Breast with
Bourbon Pan Gravy, 106–107
Pecan Tarts, 111
Twice-Baked Potatoes with
Herbs, 110

**L**
**Lamb**
Lamb Patties with Yogurt
Sauce, 100
Moroccan Lamb Chops, 115
Pan-Roasted Lamb Chops, 36
Pan-Seared Lamb Chops with
Balsamic Glaze, 122
Roast Rack of Lamb in Parsley-
Thyme Crust, 27
Lamb Patties with Yogurt Sauce,
100
Lemon-Crusted Haddock with
Cornichon Mayonnaise, 139
Lemon-Dill Zucchini, 83
Lemon-Garlic Vinaigrette, 51
Lemon Meringue Pie, 38–39
Lemon-Roasted Chicken Thighs,
136
Lime Cheesecake with Fresh Fruit,
70

**M**
Mango-Glazed Green Beans, 18
**Market-Fresh Meals**, 48–55
Chicken with Orange, Rosemary
and Nectarines, 50
Grilled Sirloin Steak with Sweet
Onion and Bell Pepper
Topping, 48
Pasta with Spicy Italian Sausage
and Mushrooms, 51
Pilaf-Stuffed Eggplant with
Mozzarella and Tomatoes, 52
Pistachio Ice Cream, 54
Mauna Kea Chocolate Cake,
150–151
Middle Eastern Pita Salad, 74
Miso-Glazed Salmon, 102
Moroccan Lamb Chops, 115
**Mushrooms**
Cheddar-Portobello Mushroom
Skillet, 114
Easy Beef Stroganoff, 19
Mushroom-Tomato Pasta with
Arugula, 140
Pan-Seared Steaks with
Mushroom-Cognac Sauce, 11
Pasta with Spicy Italian Sausage
and Mushrooms, 51
Pork Medallions with
Mushrooms and Rosemary,
148
Mushroom-Tomato Pasta with
Arugula, 140
Mu Shu Vegetable Wraps, 67

**N**
**No Stress Dinners**, 144–151
Hearty Pasta with Tomatoes and
Garbanzo Beans, 144
Mauna Kea Chocolate Cake,
150–151
Orange-Glazed Chicken, 146
Pork Medallions with
Mushrooms and Rosemary,
148
Strip Steaks with Shallots, 147

**O**
Old-Fashioned New York
Cheesecake with Strawberry
Glaze, 14–15
Orange Gingerbread with Citrus
Cream, 96
Orange-Glazed Chicken, 146

**P**
Pan-Roasted Lamb Chops, 36
Pan-Seared Lamb Chops with
Balsamic Glaze, 122
Pan-Seared Steaks with
Mushroom-Cognac Sauce, 11
Parmesan-Crusted Tomatoes, 83
**Pasta**
Hearty Pasta with Tomatoes and
Garbanzo Beans, 144
Mushroom-Tomato Pasta with
Arugula, 140
Pasta with Spicy Italian Sausage
and Mushrooms, 51
Pasta with Tomatoes and
Cannellini Beans, 101
Penne with Sausage and
Broccoli Raab, 92
Sautéed Shrimp and Pasta with
Sugar Snap Peas, 59
Shrimp and Fennel over

Linguine, 154
Tortellini Stew with Spinach and
Tomato, 124
Pasta with Spicy Italian Sausage
and Mushrooms, 51
Pasta with Tomatoes and
Cannellini Beans, 101
**Peaches**
Pork Chops with Peaches and
Basil, 80
Warm Chicken Salad with Fresh
Peaches, 64
**Pears**
Triple Ginger-Pear Bread
Pudding, 126
**Peas**
Pimiento-Topped Snow Peas, 18
Sautéed Shrimp and Pasta with
Sugar Snap Peas, 59
Pecan Tarts, 111
Penne with Sausage and Broccoli
Raab, 92
**Peppers, bell**
Grilled Sirloin Steak with Sweet
Onion and Bell Pepper
Topping, 48
Grilled Summer Vegetables, 43
Sausage and Peppers in Spanish
Rice, 82
Pepper-Smothered Skirt Steak,
138
Personal Meat Loaf, 152–153
**Pies**
Bumbleberry Pie, 30
Chocolate-Espresso Fudge Pie,
118
Lemon Meringue Pie, 38–39
Pilaf-Stuffed Eggplant with
Mozzarella and Tomatoes, 52
Pimiento-Topped Snow Peas, 18
**Pineapple**
Grilled Caramel Pineapple, 67
Vanilla Ice Cream with Broiled
Pineapple, 35
Pistachio Ice Cream, 54
**Pizza**
Grilled Pizza Margherita, 43
**Pork**
Balsamic Pork Chops and
Peppers, 10
Grilled Pork Chops with Cuban
Mojo Sauce, 56
Pork Chops with Cranberry-
Sage Chutney, 128
Pork Chops with Peaches and
Basil, 80
Pork Chops with Tarragon-
Mustard Sauce, 16
Pork Medallions with
Mushrooms and Rosemary,
148
Red Curry Pork Tenderloin, 123
Smoked Pork Chops with
Spiced Raisin Chutney, 94
Spinach Salad with Grilled Pork
Tenderloin and Strawberry
Vinaigrette, 58
Stir-Fried Orange Pork, 66
Pork Chops with Cranberry-Sage
Chutney, 128
Pork Chops with Peaches and
Basil, 80
Pork Chops with Tarragon-
Mustard Sauce, 16
Pork Medallions with Mushrooms
and Rosemary, 148
**Potatoes**
Clam and Potato Chowder, 130
Coconut-Curry Chicken and

Potatoes, 98
Grilled Potatoes with Malt Vinegar, 43
Twice-Baked Cheddar Melts, 83
Twice-Baked Potatoes with Herbs, 110
**Pudding**
Caramel Apple Bread Pudding, 86
Chocolate Omnipotence, 142
Roasted Banana Bread Pudding with Bourbon-Praline Sauce, 156–157
Triple Ginger-Pear Bread Pudding, 126
Violet Berry Fool, 78

**R**
Raspberries. *See* Berries
Red Curry Pork Tenderloin, 123
**Relish**
Ginger Cranberry-Kumquat Relish, 109
**Rhubarb**
Warm Rhubarb Sundaes, 10
**Rice**
Sausage and Peppers in Spanish Rice, 82
Roasted Banana Bread Pudding with Bourbon-Praline Sauce, 156–157
Roast Fennel with Olive Tapenade, 18
Roast Rack of Lamb in Parsley-Thyme Crust, 27

**S**
**Salads**
Grilled Honey Mustard Chicken Salad, 26
Middle Eastern Pita Salad, 74
Spinach Salad with Grilled Pork Tenderloin and Strawberry Vinaigrette, 58
Thai Beef Salad, 72
Tuna, White Bean and Tomato Salad, 84
Warm Chicken Salad with Fresh Peaches, 64
**Sauces**
Apricot & Balsamic Glazed Salmon, 116
Blackberry-Glazed Chicken Breasts, 18
Chesapeake Bay Crab Cakes with Herbed Tartar Sauce, 28
Chicken in Mojo Pan Sauce, 8
Chicken with Spicy Fresh Tomato Sauce, 83
Chimichurri Beef Steak, 42
Grilled Pork Chops with Cuban Mojo Sauce, 56
Halibut Steak with Lemon Glaze, 32
Herb-Brined Turkey Breast with Bourbon Pan Gravy, 106–107
Lamb Patties with Yogurt Sauce, 100
Lemon-Crusted Haddock with Cornichon Mayonnaise, 139
Mu Shu Vegetable Wraps, 67
Old-Fashioned New York Cheesecake with Strawberry Glaze, 14–15
Orange-Glazed Chicken, 146
Pan-Seared Lamb Chops with

Balsamic Glaze, 122
Pan-Seared Steaks with Mushroom-Cognac Sauce, 11
Pasta with Spicy Italian Sausage and Mushrooms, 51
Pilaf-Stuffed Eggplant with Mozzarella and Tomatoes, 52
Pork Chops with Tarragon-Mustard Sauce, 16
Roasted Banana Bread Pudding with Bourbon-Praline Sauce, 156–157
Turkey Burgers with Mint-Yogurt Sauce, 60
**Sausage**
Pasta with Spicy Italian Sausage and Mushrooms, 51
Penne with Sausage and Broccoli Raab, 92
Sausage and Peppers in Spanish Rice, 82
Sausage and Peppers in Spanish Rice, 82
Sautéed Shrimp and Pasta with Sugar Snap Peas, 59
Sesame-Garlic Sirloin Steak, 120
Sesame oil, 123
Shortcut Strawberry Shortcake, 10
Shrimp and Artichoke Frittata, 68
Shrimp and Fennel over Linguine, 154
**Small Effort, Large Payoff**, 72–79
Chicken Saltimbocca, 74
Cornmeal-Crusted Scallops with Corn Relish, 76
Grilled Shrimp Wraps, 75
Thai Beef Salad, 72
Violet Berry Fool, 78
**Small is Beautiful**, 152–157
Personal Meat Loaf, 152–153
Roasted Banana Bread Pudding with Bourbon-Praline Sauce, 156–157
Shrimp and Fennel over Linguine, 154
Smoked Pork Chops with Spiced Raisin Chutney, 94
Snapper in Parchment, 20
Soups and stews
Clam and Potato Chowder, 130
Tortellini Stew with Spinach and Tomato, 124
Spice-Grilled Sirloin Steaks, 36
**Spice is Nice**, 90–97
Buttermilk Pan-Fried Chicken, 93
Huevos Rancheros Tostadas, 90
Orange Gingerbread with Citrus Cream, 96
Penne with Sausage and Broccoli Raab, 92
Smoked Pork Chops with Spiced Raisin Chutney, 94
**Spinach**
Spinach Salad with Grilled Pork Tenderloin and Strawberry Vinaigrette, 58
Tortellini Stew with Spinach and Tomato, 124
Spinach Salad with Grilled Pork Tenderloin and Strawberry Vinaigrette, 58
**Spring Fling**, 24–30
Bumbleberry Pie, 30
Chesapeake Bay Crab Cakes with Herbed Tartar Sauce, 28
Grilled Honey Mustard Chicken Salad, 26

Grilled Porterhouse Steak with Herb Butter, 24
Roast Rack of Lamb in Parsley-Thyme Crust, 27
**Squash**
Browned Butter, Honey and Sage, 115
Maple-Bacon Topping, 115
Marmalade and Jalapeño, 115
**Steak Medley**, 32–39
Asparagus-Goat Cheese Omelet, 35
Chicken with Olives, Tomatoes and Parsley, 34
Halibut Steak with Lemon Glaze, 32
Lemon Meringue Pie, 38–39
Pan-Roasted Lamb Chops, 36
Spice-Grilled Sirloin Steaks, 36
Stir-Fried Orange Pork, 66
**Stir-fry**
Stir-Fried Orange Pork, 66
Thai Shrimp Stir-Fry, 12
Strawberries. *See* Berries
Strawberry-Orange Sundaes, 35
Strip Steaks with Shallots, 147
**Summer Kitchen**, 40–47
Chimichurri Beef Steak, 42
Citrus Grilled Chicken, 44
Frozen Lemon-Lime Mousse with Berries, 46
Gorgonzola Toasts on the Grill, 43
Grilled Mini Meat Loaves, 40
Grilled Pizza Margherita, 43
**Summer Suppers**, 64–71
Lime Cheesecake with Fresh Fruit, 70
Mu Shu Vegetable Wraps, 67
Shrimp and Artichoke Frittata, 68
Stir-Fried Orange Pork, 66
Warm Chicken Salad with Fresh Peaches, 64
Sunday Supper Chicken, 132
**Suppers that Sizzle**, 56–63
Grilled Pork Chops with Cuban Mojo Sauce, 56
Sautéed Shrimp and Pasta with Sugar Snap Peas, 59
Spinach Salad with Grilled Pork Tenderloin and Strawberry Vinaigrette, 58
Turkey Burgers with Mint-Yogurt Sauce, 60

**T**
**Tarts**
Pecan Tarts, 111
Warm Chocolate Truffle Tart, 134
Thai Beef Salad, 72
Thai Shrimp Stir-Fry, 12
**Tomatoes**
Chicken with Olives, Tomatoes and Parsley, 34
Chicken with Spicy Fresh Tomato Sauce, 83
Hearty Pasta with Tomatoes and Garbanzo Beans, 144
Mushroom-Tomato Pasta with Arugula, 140
Parmesan-Crusted Tomatoes, 83
Pasta with Tomatoes and Cannellini Beans, 101
Tortellini Stew with Spinach and Tomato, 124
Tuna, White Bean and Tomato

Salad, 84
Tortellini Stew with Spinach and Tomato, 124
Triple Ginger-Pear Bread Pudding, 126
Tuna, White Bean and Tomato Salad, 84
**Turkey**
Herb-Brined Turkey Breast with Bourbon Pan Gravy, 106–107
Turkey Burgers with Mint-Yogurt Sauce, 60
Turkey Burgers with Mint-Yogurt Sauce, 60
Twice-Baked Cheddar Melts, 83
Twice-Baked Potatoes with Herbs, 110

**V**
Vanilla Ice Cream with Broiled Pineapple, 35
**Vinaigrette**
Chunky Blue Cheese Vinaigrette, 51
Fresh Herb Vinaigrette, 51
Herbed Olive Oil Vinaigrette, 26
Lemon-Garlic Vinaigrette, 51
Spinach Salad with Grilled Pork Tenderloin and Strawberry Vinaigrette, 58
Warm Chicken Salad with Fresh Peaches, 64
Violet Berry Fool, 78

**W**
**Warm and Comforting**, 136–143
Chocolate Omnipotence, 142
Lemon-Crusted Haddock with Cornichon Mayonnaise, 139
Lemon-Roasted Chicken Thighs, 136
Mushroom-Tomato Pasta with Arugula, 140
Pepper-Smothered Skirt Steak, 138
Warm Chicken Salad with Fresh Peaches, 64
Warm Chocolate Truffle Tart, 134
Warm Rhubarb Sundaes, 10
**Wraps**
Grilled Shrimp Wraps, 75
Mu Shu Vegetable Wraps, 67

**Z**
**Zucchini**
Grilled Summer Vegetables, 43
Lemon-Dill Zucchini, 83